STUDIES IN PHILOSOPHY

XXIV

SPINOZA'S PHILOSOPHY OF LAW

by

GAIL BELAIEF

1971
MOUTON
THE HAGUE · PARIS

© Copyright 1971 in The Netherlands.
Mouton & Co., N.V., Publishers, The Hague.

No part of this book may be translated or reproduced in any form, by print, photoprint, microfilm, or any other means, without written permission from the publishers.

LIBRARY OF CONGRESS CATALOG CARD NUMBER: 78-118275

Printed in The Netherlands by P. H. Klop N.V., Printers, The Hague.

PREFACE

The purpose of this work is firstly to develop in systematic form a philosophy of law based on scattered suggestions found throughout Spinoza's philosophical writings; and secondly to analyze the possible significance of Spinoza's thought with respect to problems of legal theory in general. In order adequately to formulate Spinoza's position and do justice to the intention of his remarks, it is necessary to place his theory of law within the wider framework of his metaphysical and ethical philosophy. If Spinoza's philosophical perspective and orientation are disregarded it is too easy, for example, to construe him as an inconsistent Hobbesian with respect to his legal and political philosophy.

The exposition of Spinoza's theory as well as the more general discussion of the problems of legal theory is centered for the most part around the question of the relation of civil law to a higher law, the moral law or the natural law or both. Since Spinoza's notion of the natural law is significantly different from the traditional conception,[1] his legal philosophy is not developed within the framework of classical natural law theory although certain limited comparisons are made.

The first three chapters are primarily expository: Chapter I deals with a presentation of Spinoza's notion of civil law. The annotation is offered less as a 'proof' of the analysis than as a guide to what can be found in Spinoza's writings. Chapter II formulates Spinoza's conception of the natural law, including a discussion of natural right, the Divine law, and the ceremonial law. The discussion of

[1] For a discussion of the traditional conception of natural law, cf. Appendix A.

ceremonial law is included both for the sake of completeness in the presentation of the different types of law and as an example of a legal system which shares certain characteristics of civil law. Spinoza's ethical theory is outlined in Chapter III as a basis for discussing the relation of civil law to moral law and the different question of the evaluation of civil law.

The discussion of the relation between civil law and a higher law, both the natural and the moral law, in Chapter IV introduces the critical appraisal of Spinoza's legal theory with respect to the consistency of certain of his fundamental principles. Chapter V deals with an analysis of six problems or issues of legal philosophy and suggests possible areas in which Spinoza's insights and general approach might be relevant to their solution. The issues discussed are the problem of the evaluation of law; the problem of the source of law; the problem of judicial legislation; the problem of stability and change in the law; the problem of the limits to sovereignty and the jurisdiction of laws; and the problem of the end of law and of the duty of the subject and the sovereign.

Reference to works written about Spinoza is avoided because of the belief that isolated remarks concerning commentators would not be of general interest, nor could they do justice to the writers so considered. Furthermore the literature on Spinoza's legal philosophy in very sparse indeed and not altogether satisfactory in the depth of its analysis. The primary references are indicated below.[2]

---

[2] Duff, *Spinoza's Political and Ethical Philosophy;* H. Cairns, "Spinoza's Theory of Law"; H. Lauterpacht, "Spinoza and International Law"; Pollock, "Spinoza's Political Doctrine with Special Regard to his Relation to English Publicists"; H. A. Wolfson, *The Philosophy of Spinoza;* and C. E. Vaughan, *Studies in the History of Political Philosophy.* For fuller information on these sources and for further references, see Bibliography.

CONTENTS

Preface 5

Introduction: The Concept of Law in General 9

I. The Concept of Civil Law in Spinoza 13
   A. The Definition of Civil Law 13
   B. The Instrumentality of Law 15
   C. The Limits of Legal Jurisdiction 17
   D. Obedience to Law 20
   E. The Connection between the Validity and Efficacy of a Law 25
   F. Law as the Will of the Sovereign 27
   G. International Law 29
   H. Law as a Means of the State 31

II. The Natural Divine Law; The Natural Law; Natural Right; and Ceremonial Law in Spinoza 34
   A. The Natural Divine Law 34
   B. The Law of the Prophets or the Ceremonial Law . 38
   C. The Natural Law 41
   D. Human Laws 43
   E. The Natural Laws of Human Nature 44
   F. Natural Right 49

III. The Ethical Dimension and the Moral Law in Spinoza 54
   A. Two Apparent Difficulties with the Notion of a Moral Law 54

CONTENTS

B. The Meaning of Morality 56
C. The Rational Principle and Freedom 58
D. The Moral Law as Law Improper 61
E. Relation to the Natural Divine Law 62
F. Key to Relations among Men 64
G. The Sphere of Relevance of the Moral Law . . . 67
H. Certain Difficulties Reconsidered 69

IV. The Relation Between Civil Law and a Higher Law in Spinoza 72
A. General Considerations 72
B. The End of Civil Law 75
C. The Validity of a Civil Law 77
D. The Duty of the Subject and of the Sovereign . . 84
E. The Relation between Law and Morality 88

V. Problems of Legal Theory 100
A. The Problem of the Evaluation of Law 100
B. The Problem of the Source of Law 104
C. The Problem of Judicial Legislation 107
D. The Problem of Stability and Change in the Law . 110
E. The Problem of the Limits to Sovereignty and the Jurisdiction of Law 113
F. The Problem of the End of Law and of the Duty of the Subject and the Sovereign 116
G. Conclusion 122

Appendix A Notes on the Classical Doctrine of Natural Law 126

Appendix B Latin Quotations from Spinoza 136

Selected Bibliography 142

Index 148

INTRODUCTION:
THE CONCEPT OF LAW IN GENERAL

The widest notion of law which Spinoza offers is that which emphasizes regularity of behavior: "The word law, taken in the abstract, means that by which each individual, or all things, or some things of a particular species, act in one and the same certain and definite manner, which manner depends either on natural necessity or human decree."[1] Laws which depend on natural necessity are the natural Divine law and the natural law; those which depend on human decree are the civil law and positive Divine law or ceremonial law.[2]

The definition of law is further qualified in two different ways, alternately excluding human law on the one hand and the natural Divine law and the natural law on the other hand from the class of proper laws: First Spinoza notes that "A law which depends on human decree, and which is more correctly called an ordinance is one which men have laid down for themselves and others in order to live more safely and conveniently, or for other reasons."[3] That is, human laws are not laws proper; they do not belong to the class of laws but rather to the class of ordinances. Only laws depending

---

[1] Carl Gebhardt, *Spinoza Opera* (Heidelberg, Carl Winters), Vol. III, p. 57, 1. 23-27. *Tractatus Theologico-Politicus,* Chap. 4. Original translation. Spinoza's original Latin of quotations whose translation gave any difficulty is given in Appendix B. In the text, each footnote from Spinoza notes the corresponding page in Gebhardt's *Opera,* designated as "G", followed by the volume number and page. The lines in Gebhardt are also noted for those quotations included in Appendix B.
[2] Cf. Chapter 2, Section D, for a discussion of the propriety of Spinoza's distinction between natural necessity and other causal modes, e.g., human agency.
[3] *TPT,* Chap. 4. G. Vol. III, p. 57, 1. 28-31. Original translation.

on natural necessity belong to the class of laws. However Spinoza also states that "The word law seems to be only applied to natural things by analogy, and is commonly taken to signify a command which men can either enact or neglect."[4] That is, the Divine and natural laws are quasi-laws if law proper is taken to designate commands which can either be obeyed or neglected. Spinoza makes no distinction in the text between ordinances and commands which could explain his claim that on the one hand human laws, being ordinances, are not laws, and on the other hand natural laws, not being commands, are not laws. The implication is that Spinoza is dealing with two quite different notions of law proper: with respect to the original formulation of law as regulating behavior in a 'fixed and definite manner' the immutable natural and natural Divine laws are certainly candidates whereas human law, not guaranteeing obedience, would be law only by analogy. With respect to the notion of law as command, implying mutability and human agency, human laws are paradigmatic and the natural and natural Divine laws are laws only by analogy. A decision at this point regarding Spinoza's notion of the nature or essence of law could be only arbitrary.

Following this Spinoza limits the extension of the concept 'law' 'more particularly' to products of human promulgation: "Law seems to be defined more particularly as a plan of life laid down by man for himself or others with a certain end."[5] This notion of law as a plan of life promulgated by men denies natural and natural Divine law the status of law proper. In a final attempt to generalize the notion of law (as a plan of life) to include both the natural Divine law and human law, Spinoza states that, "Law (*lex*) then, being a plan of living which *men* have for a certain object laid down for themselves or others, may, as it seems, be divided into *human law and Divine law*."[6] The text indicates that Spinoza is referring to the natural Divine law insofar as it is a universal law and does not depend on the truth of historical narratives. The conjunction of the

---

[4] *Ibid.*, Chap. 4. G. Vol. III, p. 58, 1. 28-31. Original translation.
[5] *TPT*, Chap. 4. G. Vol. III, p. 58, 1. 33-35. Original translation.
[6] *The Chief Works of Benedict de Spinoza, Theological-Political Treatise*, Vol. I, trans. R. H. M. Elwes (N. Y., Dover Publications, 1955), p. 59, Chap. 4. G. Vol. III, p. 59.

notion of law as a plan of living which men have laid down with the notion of the natural Divine law (i.e., the law of God) is difficult to reconcile. Since the prior definition of law as a plan of life also noted that it was laid down by men it is probable that Spinoza is taking human law as the paradigm, i.e., law as a command or ordinance, and inconsistently attempts to include natural Divine law, which he points out quite definitively is not a command at all.[7]

Although it is impossible on the basis of Spinoza's general remarks, noted above, to give a coherent definition of law in general, the ambiguities of the general discussion are clarified to an extent by Spinoza's subsequent analysis of the particular types of laws. The further discussion recognizes human laws as laws proper and the natural and natural Divine laws as quasi-laws. The basic distinction here is between commands which can be obeyed or disobeyed and which function coercively, and 'formulas' which relate to the events of the natural world. The natural and natural Divine laws are not commands imposed on the natural world — thus their analogical character — but rather embody the events of the natural process itself. Spinoza is, in short, more sympathetic to the notion of law as a command which is imposed on behavior than law as an intrinsic part of that behavior itself. The notion of regulation of behavior, although broad enough to include natural and human law, suffers from equivocation if one recognizes the very different modes of regulation involved. It is possible that a tacit recognition of this point is partially responsible for Spinoza's fluctuating account of the essence of law — alternately stressing on the one hand the command aspect and on the other hand stressing the aspect of natural necessity as characteristic of law.

The various types of laws will be discussed within the framework which Spinoza offers. For example, Spinoza speaks of the natural Divine law as law as a plan of living and as regulatory of behavior, and notes also that it is pseudo-law (with reference to the definition of law as a command). It will be taken as recognized that this ambiguity is present.

[7] Cf. Chapter 2, Section A.

I

THE CONCEPT OF CIVIL LAW IN SPINOZA

A. THE DEFINITION OF CIVIL LAW

For Spinoza the supreme end of the civil state[1] is to institute conditions of peace and security of life in which men can achieve 'true excellence of the mind'. The state does not exist for the single purpose of making its citizens obey its laws. Law, however, is the principal means by which the state can achieve its end and for this reason the legal system of a state assumes central importance.

In its widest significance, civil law, for Spinoza, is an agency of social control which can be distinguished from other agencies of the state by what could be called its instrumentality, its mode of functioning. Spinoza defines human law as a "plan of living which serves only to render life and the state secure",[2] that is, law stipulates the characteristic structure of the particular state and has a definite aim and function. Law as both a tool of the state and that which characterizes the organization of the state is the conception which will be analyzed below.

The distinction between civil law, taken as an institution of the state, and other agencies within the state, for example, religious or social institutions, is that law is a command issued by the sovereign to the citizens, who, as subjects, are bound to execute these commands of their ruler.

---

[1] The civil state, for Spinoza, has its foundations in the fact that men, discovering they can better achieve material security and initiate intellectual and moral development, join together, with or without a prior contract, to form a civil community.
[2] *TPT, op. cit.,* p. 59, Chap. 4. G. Vol. III, p. 59.

Rewards and punishments are adjoined to the law as expressive of this compulsive aspect. "In consequence, law is apt to be regarded as a rule of life prescribed for men by the command of others; accordingly, those who obey law are said to live under law, and are thought to be slaves."[3] Thus civil law is a command issued by the sovereign with sanctions expressive of its compulsive aspect. Although Spinoza has outlined the basic elements of the command theory of law, it is contended in this analysis that this resemblance is merely formal and that the intention of Spinoza's theory is essentially different from that of the classical command theory. The command aspect of civil law is intrinsically tied up with the manner in which laws function. Law must involve a coercive aspect if it is to be regulative of men's behavior insofar as men, for the most part, do not recognize the necessary function and value of law. Although Spinoza does repeatedly characterize law as a command or order of the sovereign, this characterization is not so much expressive of the essence of law as it is a consequence of the lack of intrinsic appeal of most laws to those who are subject to them.

Spinoza, in characterizing civil law as a command, emphasizes a significant distinction from what he calls natural law and natural Divine law which are not commands in the proper signification of the term.[4] Natural Divine laws and natural laws are necessary principles of existence which can neither be obeyed nor disobeyed in the strict sense, nor are they products of human invention. Natural Divine law carries eternal truth, descriptive of what occurs of necessity in the universe on the basis of God's will which is identical with his understanding. Spinoza's notion of natural law is not in the tradition which conceives the natural law as a natural moral law stipulating the good and bad, just and unjust aspects of human behavior.[5] Natural law relates to the processes of nature and is neutral with respect to value parameters. When it is noted that

---

[3] *Benedict de Spinoza: The Political Works,* trans. A. G. Wernham (Oxford, The Clarendon Press, 1958); *A Treatise on Religion and Politics* (TPT), p. 69, Chap. 4. G. Vol. III, p. 59, 1. 8-10.
[4] For a detailed treatment of Divine and natural law cf. Chap. II, Section A and C.
[5] For a discussion of the natural law tradition cf. Appendix A.

events take place by natural necessity, this is acknowledged as a fact of behavior with which civil law must deal and is not taken as a direct moral requirement of the coincidence or compatibility of the civil law. Civil law, on the other hand, is the product of human will, which is not *ipso facto* determinative of actual occurrences, although it may and should be expressive of human reason. Human law can be either obeyed or neglected, the command accepted as regulative of behavior or not.

In order for civil law to achieve efficacy the citizens must be induced in some way to obey the substance of the command. "As the true object of legislation is only perceived by a few ... legislators, with a view to exacting general obedience, have wisely put forward another object."[6] The condition of efficacy is of central importance for the development of Spinoza's notion of law. It determines the manner in which citizens can be led to obey and derivatively determines the sphere of control exercisable by the civil state, that is, the behavior to which obedience can be demanded. Analysis of the instrumentality of law will give insight into the limits of legal control and thus of the legal jurisdiction of the state.

B. THE INSTRUMENTALITY OF LAW

In analyzing the way in which law functions in leading citizens to obey the substance of a legal command, it is necessary to consider aspects of Spinoza's theory of human behavior. According to Spinoza, since the intellect can never achieve absolute authority over the emotions a person is always motivated to a certain extent by passion. Men inevitably seek their own interests and advantage, partially in accordance with reason, but primarily as guided by impulses which are rooted in the object as desired. Men who have not achieved full rationality make frequent errors regarding their real interests and the proper means of attaining satisfaction. In this condition of partial rationality is located both the need for laws,

---

[6] Elwes, *TPT,* p. 58, Chap. 4. G. Vol. III, pp. 58-59.

viz., to enable men who are led by contrary desires to live in harmony with each other in order to achieve better conditions of life, and the manner in which law can 'work' as a command. That is to say, in order for a particular law to function, to induce men to obey its dictates with a recognizable minimum of efficacy, it must appeal to men on the level of desire and self-interest. If a citizen did not feel that obeying a particular law was to his advantage he would not do so. Nor could he be convinced through arguments of reason unless they were such as also affect the emotions. Laws must be not only for the good or advantage of the citizens but must at the same time appeal to them as such. The further question as to the important relation between the efficacy of a law and its validity will be considered below. At this point it may be noted that the efficacy of a law depends for Spinoza on what it does, its content, and not on who instituted it or how it is enforced.

The legislator, whether he is a monarch or the whole people, is not able to force the subjects to desire what is against their inclination, 'things which cause indignation in the majority'. Given this as a law of human nature it occurs that the lawgiver must devise special means of persuasion if he is to institute legislation seemingly at variance with the instincts and desires of his citizens. It is for this reason that it is necessary to attach rewards and punishments to laws;[7] men will then appreciate that obedience is to their advantage. The state must claim the power "of promulgating laws and supporting them, not by reason, which cannot restrain the emotions, . . . but by penalties."[8]

---

[7] Spinoza appears to give a utilitarian justification of punishment. In Letter 78 to Oldenburg (A. Wolf, *The Correspondence of Spinoza* (N.Y., Dial Press, 1927)) he writes, "He who is unable to control his desires and to restrain them through fear of the laws . . . must be excused for his weakness . . ." G. Vol. IV, p. 327.

[8] Spinoza, *Ethics,* ed. James Gutmann (N. Y., Hafner Publishing Co., 1957), Part 4, Prop. 37, Note 2. All subsequent references to the *Ethics* are to this edition and will be designated "E". G. Vol. II, p. 238.

C. THE LIMITS OF LEGAL JURISDICTION

As noted above, the analysis of the mode of functioning of law indicates the limits of effective legal action of the state. Because men can be persuaded to obey a particular law only if it appeals to them as advantageous, it will be possible to legislate solely on those matters which appear desirable or to which sanctions can be attached as adequate incentives. As Spinoza understands the situation, "He who seeks to regulate everything by law, is more likely to arouse vices than to reform them."[9] An important example of this is the question of laws against freedom of thought and speech. For Spinoza there could be no way of enforcing such a law in a commonwealth since it could never be shown to be to one's advantage to have opinions and beliefs subjected to external control. In accordance with one of the fundamental laws of human nature, the power to think excludes all outward compulsion; thus man must judge for himself and he can never, according to another law of human nature, judge it to be advantageous to have his thoughts and speech under external coercion. "If a sovereign were to command a subject to hate someone who has bound him by a service, or to love someone who has done him harm, if he were to command him not to take offence at insults, not to desire to rid himself of fear, and not to feel the many other emotions of this kind which follow necessarily from the laws of human nature, he would command in vain."[10] To say merely, 'The state so commands' can never be a reason to obey, unless obedience can be made to seem the greater good.

Obviously, in actual practice, the penalties attached to many particularly unlikely laws can be made great enough to act as a stimulus for obedience although at the same time such an attempt may initiate revolutionary movements. These extremes notwithstanding, Spinoza contends that it is unquestionably wiser, for the security, peace and solidarity of the state, to structure laws so that

---

[9] Elwes, *TPT*, p. 261, Chap. 20. G. Vol. III, p. 243.
[10] *TPT*, Chap. 17. G. Vol. III, p. 201, 1. 16-21. Original translation.

the citizens obey out of hope rather than fear. "It is true that quarrels which arise between parents and children are generally more frequent and more bitter than quarrels between masters and slaves, yet it is not conducive to good family management to make the father a master, and to treat children as slaves."[11] It is the duty and obligation of a subject to obey the laws, and the state must aim at making this obedience as natural as possible. This is the responsibility of the lawgiver as well as the natural necessity of the state. If the state does not meet a minimum level of reasonableness in its commands, it cannot expect nor gain the obedience of its citizens, no matter what penalties it attaches to its laws. There are certain things a man cannot do; essentially he cannot desire to do anything which he does not understand to be to his advantage, whether he is right or wrong. This may be taken as the natural limit to the authority of the state. The greatness of a state is thus not exhibited by its ability to punish, its power to maintain itself through threats, but rather by that reasonableness and 'rightness" which renders enforcement of its punishments and threats superfluous. A state which does not perform its given functions characterizes itself as a weak state which is more a prison than a sanctuary in its duplication of the aggressions it was instituted to dissolve.

The state must inspire confidence and hope by instituting laws which the subjects desire to obey; yet these laws must not be directed exclusively to the unreasoned level of desire prevalent in the multitude. The solution of this apparent antinomy focuses the job of legislative wisdom which must raise the citizens to a higher understanding of the needs of the state, in fact, of the need FOR the state, and of themselves as members of that commonwealth. Although the good can be manifested on the lower levels of desire, the state cannot be satisfied with aiming its laws at this level, for example, the satisfaction of the desire for sensual gratification. It must rather work on this level as a means of bringing men to a higher achievement. The laws must promise to each what he desires, for example, better physical conditions of life, but they must

---

[11] *Benedict de Spinoza: The Political Works,* trans. A. G. Wernham (Oxford, The Clarendon Press, 1958); *A Treatise on Politics* (PT), p. 317, Chap. 6, Sect. 4. G. Vol. III, p. 298, 1. 20-23.

do this in such a way that obedience to the laws will bring men closer to the true good. The laws of the state do not aim at destroying man's natural impulse but rather at allowing him to satisfy this impulse to persevere in his being, which he could not do without membership in a civil state. As Vaughan puts it, it is a question of "enlightened as against blind self interest".[12] If the citizens can be brought to obey from an understanding of the benefits of law rather than from fear of punishment, the state has, through its laws, increased the harmony and the stability of the state, and has thereby more closely approached the fulfillment of its purpose.

This is not to say that spiritual improvement or private blessedness as true goods can or should be legislated. For Spinoza, law has only to do with the control of external acts, not with the state of mind or motivation of the citizen. It cannot be the job of the state to make men moral or religious since the jurisdiction of legal authority does not extend to these spheres. Ultimately all that the state can do directly is to make men obedient to its laws and this within certain limits. "For the mind, so far as it makes use of reason, is dependent, not on the supreme authorities, but on itself."[13] As morality and religion have to do with the development of the mind and character of an individual, his beliefs and level of understanding, civil law can have no direct control of this. Law can and should structure society in a way that is conducive to the development of religion and morality in the individual but its control cannot extend over an individual's beliefs and opinions. If we take the distinction between public and private spheres, law can be said to have control of any public, i.e., overt, act, including ethical or religious 'acts', but it can have no control of the individual in his private capacity, i.e., his mental activities. "For by what rewards or threats can a man be brought to believe, that the whole is not greater than its part, or that God does not exist . . . or generally anything contrary to his sense or thought . . . And to this head must likewise be

---

[12] C. E. Vaughan, *Studies in the History of Political Philosophy* (Manchester, The University Press, 1925).
[13] *The Chief Works of Benedict de Spinoza; A Political Treatise*, trans. R. H. M. Elwes (N. Y., Dover Publications), Vol. I, p. 317, Chap. 3, Sect. 10. G. Vol. III, p. 288.

referred such things as are so abhorrent to human nature, that it regards them as actually worse than any evil, as that a man should be witness against himself, or torture himself . . . or not strive to avoid death, and the like . . .".[14]

D. OBEDIENCE TO LAW

From the point of view of the rights of the commonwealth, the citizen has an absolute duty to obey its laws. Spinoza does not exhibit the naivete of ignoring the fact that some of these laws might be bad laws. Holding the criteria for judging laws in abeyance, it is of interest to determine the source of this absolute duty of obedience. The institution of a legal structure in a state is the means to the achievement of the freedom of the individual, the development of the powers of reason latent in human nature. By means of this structure, individuals are brought into contact with each other as partners in a common endeavor rather than as antagonists seeking their own gratification to the detriment of the other. "In the civil state all fear the same things, and all have the same ground of security . . .".[15]

Each citizen of a commonwealth, it is true, will always seek his own interest — according to Spinoza, a man has no other choice. The important difference is that in a civil state each one's interests are so closely and irrevocably tied up with the others that by pursuing his own advantage he will further that of his fellow men. In terms of the laws of the state this means that each finds it to his advantage to obey the laws — if only to avoid punishment — and in so doing raises himself above the level of narrowly understood self interest by the fact that his act of obedience strengthens the state, maintenance of which is to the advantage of all. In pursuing their own advantage men will no longer be as enemies but, as it were, as one mind acting in concert to establish the security and peace of the state. For Spinoza this is the basis of individual freedom; "a

---

[14] Elwes, *PT*, p. 304. Chap. 3. Sect. 8. G. Vol. III, p. 287.
[15] *Ibid.*, p. 302, Chap. 3, Sect. 3. G. Vol. III, p. 285.

man (is) so far free as he is led by reason".[16] "Finally, the political order is naturally established to remove general fear and to dispel general suffering, and thus its chief aim is one which every rational man would try to promote in the state of nature; though his efforts in that state would be useless." [17] As each man seeks his preservation and self-affirmation he is led closer to his true self, which is reason. It is only in the civil state that reason can be developed. Outside the civil state man, as his own guardian and protector, is by circumstances forced to remain on the level of gratification of his passions in order to satisfy the first level of his needs. According to Spinoza, "When each man seeks most that which is profitable to himself, then are men most profitable to one another",[18] because each, in seeking his true advantage will endeavor to live according to the guidance of reason. Spinoza states that "Whatever causes men to live in harmony with one another, is profitable, and, on the contrary, whatever brings discord into the State is evil."[19] Thus the individual finds that in the process of working towards his own self-preservation he comes into contact with other men who constitute an integral part of this endeavor.

However as a citizen of a state one is not in a position to decide what is just or unjust, right or wrong, but must submit his will to that of the commonwealth. "Obedience is the constant will to execute what, by the general decree of the commonwealth, ought to be done." [20] This is the duty of a subject and the right of a citizen. The state is composed of a group of men who have come together for their own advantage and it is of ultimate importance for the continuance of that state that they each obey its dictates as rules of life which they have accepted. The right of "being one's own judge ceases in the civil state".[21] The decrees of the commonwealth must be taken to be the will of all, the dominion as guided by one mind; thus "however iniquitous the subject may think the common-

---

[16] *PT, op. cit.*, p. 295, Chap. 2, Sect. 11. G. Vol. III, p. 280.
[17] Wernham, PT, p. 289, Chap. 3, Sect. 6. G. Vol. III, p. 286, 1. 26-29.
[18] *E, op. cit.*, part 4, Prop. 35, Coll. 2. G. Vol. II, p. 233.
[19] *E, op. cit.*, part 4, Prop. 40. G. Vol. II, p. 241.
[20] Elwes, *PT*, p. 314, Chap. 5, Sect. 4. G. Vol. III, p. 296.
[21] *PT, op. cit.*, p. 302, Chap. 3, Sect. 3. G. Vol. III, p. 285.

wealth's decisions, he is none the less bound to execute them".[22] The subject has an absolute duty to obey the laws of the commonwealth, to submit himself to the laws as if they were products of his own will, to the furthest point of feasibility.

If the laws are evil to the extent that it appears more advantageous to incur the force of the sanction than to suffer the consequences of obedience, or, in the extreme case to disrupt the existing form of the state by disobeying its commands, the man will be unable to obey the dictum.[23] At this point it is no longer a choice of obeying or disobeying the law in question and the fact that the citizen has a duty to obey is not relevant. The duty is however absolute until this point: reason teaches that the commonwealth can maintain peace only if its dictates are obeyed. It may be necessary for the citizen to obey particular laws which he considers iniquitous if the state is to be maintained. Spinoza contends that the advantages of the state should be understood to be of such magnitude that a man will judge it to his advantage to obey any laws in order to preserve the unity and existence of the state. If one chooses, by maintaining residence and citizenship within a state, to be a subject of that commonwealth he has in so choosing incurred certain responsibilities which he must carry out if the state is to continue. If, under extreme conditions, the individual judges it to be to his advantage to forego the benefits of the state, he will be in a position to choose to disobey its laws. He thereby declares himself an enemy of the dominion and takes the consequences of individual punishment, or in the extreme situation, instigates the disruption of the existing form of the state.

In speaking of the state as one mind, Spinoza is not assuming that there is total agreement regarding the legal enactments of the state but is referring rather to the agreement of citizenship which all members have taken on themselves, and which entails ceding right of action to the authority of the government. It should be understood that advantages and disadvantages are the natural con-

---

[22] *Ibid.,* p. 302-3, Chap. 3, Sect. 5. G. Vol. III, p. 286.
[23] It can never be the case that the citizen has a LEGAL right to disobey. It would be a self-contradictory assertion to maintain that one was legally justified in disobeying a law.

sequences of this affiliation and it is against reason to balk at particular enactments which one might not approve. As indicated above, the sovereign has the absolute duty not to allow the situation to occur where it is more advantageous for a subject to disrupt the state than to obey its laws. "Contempt or breach of the laws . . . (is) not so much to be imputed to the wickedness of the subjects, as to the bad state of a dominion." [24] There is a duty for the citizen to satisfy the expectations of the sovereign and a corresponding duty for the sovereign to satisfy the hopes of the citizens, with a tacit agreement to the effect that both the subjects and the sovereign desire what is best for themselves qua members of the state. The state must be organized so that what is to the advantage of the leader is also to the advantage of his subjects. This situation, Spinoza contends, can occur only when the state is guided by reason with its laws aiming at the security of the state and of life. "A dominion must . . . be so ordered that all, governing and governed alike, whether they will or no, shall do what makes for the general welfare; that is, that all . . . shall be compelled to live according to the dictate of reason." [25] Laws should be structured in a manner that for each to realize his own desire, he must will what is to the interest of all.

If men were led solely by reason they would understand it to be to their advantage to maintain the commonwealth by general obedience to its laws. In fact if men were led solely by reason there would be no need for external control and, *a fortiori,* for the command of laws since each would do his duty willingly. However, as the multitude of men are governed more by passion than reason, each particular law must be couched in terms that appeal to them as desirable, notwithstanding the fact that obedience must also be rational. Spinoza, however, in discussing law, is not as interested in the motives for obedience, whether enlightened or unenlightened, as in the fact of obedience. "It is the constant disposition to obey, not the motive for obedience, which makes a man a subject." [26]

---

[24] *PT,* op. cit., p. 313, Chap. 5, Sect. 2. G. Vol. III, p. 295.
[25] *PT, op. cit.,* p. 316, Chap. 6, Sect. 3. G. Vol. III, pp. 297-298.
[26] *TPT,* Chap. 17. G. Vol. III, p. 202, 1. 2-3. Original translation.

However in order to make obedience to a set of laws truly profitable the laws must be rational whether or not the multitude understands them as such.

Spinoza contends that it is unquestionably better for subjects to obey the laws out of reverence and respect for them or for the personage of their promulgation than to obey the laws from fear of the consequences of disobedience. The latter condition would not be a state of peace but merely the absence of war. The state will be much stronger in the former case and the citizens freer when they are obedient to the laws from an understanding of their rightness rather than submissive from fear of their penalties. This situation can occur only when the laws are rational, that is, in accordance with the universal truths of human nature, and the subjects are convinced of the utility of the laws.

Since the strength, and for Spinoza, the goodness of a state is proportionate to the rationality of its dictums, a state can become weakened to the point of impotence by the institution of unreasonable laws. In such a situation the state can be said to do wrong — at the point where it is no longer possible for men to choose to obey the laws because obedience would initiate worse conditions than suffering the penalties attached to the iniquitous laws. However "it is very rare for sovereigns to issue commands which are utterly foolish, for their main task — if they are to safeguard themselves and retain their sovereignty — is to plan for the common good and direct everything by the dictate of reason."[27] If this situation were to occur, obedience would no longer be required or expected because it is in point of fact impossible. Men as noted above cannot act against that impulse so fundamentally ingrained in them to seek their advantage; they cannot elect to do that which is against their will. It is not necessary then for Spinoza to speak out against manifest tyranny in moralistic terms — for him such a situation, *viz.,* the enforcement of laws totally averse to human need and desire, need not be denounced in theory as it is in practice impossible of achievement. It is as if the natural laws of human nature guarantee that the individual will not be coerced against his will.

[27] Wernham, *TPT,* p. 135, Chap. 16. G. Vol. III, p. 1964, 1. 12-15.

As Cairns puts it, there is an "inescapable connection between power and its proper exercise".[28]

E. THE CONNECTION BETWEEN THE VALIDITY AND EFFICACY OF A LAW

It is generally conceded that, if a legal system exacts no, or very minimal, obedience from the citizens who are subject to its laws, at this point of negligible efficacy the validity (existence) of the set of laws is called into question. Law, no matter how its nature is conceived, is instituted to control behavior and if it has a negligible effect on conduct, it can no longer be said to function as law. Such a code would be impotent and not considered valid for the particular territory and subjects at the time in question.

Spinoza considers the more interesting question of particular laws which in practice have negligible control of conduct. He concludes that the validity of a law is dependent on whether or not it is obeyed, its efficacy. If the command of a legislator is not obeyed by the multitude it is not a law even if it is enacted and promulgated in accordance with the regulations of legal procedure. This point recognizes that the function of law is to control human behavior as both a plan of life and a command imposed on subjects. If a law does not achieve adequate control of behavior it is, as it were, paper legislation, rather than an intrinsic part of a valid legal system. This relates to Spinoza's notion of power as essentially characteristic of nature. Significant impotence destroys the nature of anything — "But the universal power of nature as a whole is simply the power of all individual things combined." [29] If anything lacks the power to function according to its essential nature, it can no longer be said to participate as the SAME thing in reality. This is as true for an individual law as it is for an entire legal system, as true for an individual man as it is for the state.

Connected with this point is Spinoza's repeated insistence that

---

[28] Huntington Cairns, "Spinoza's Theory of Law", *Columbia Law Review*, Vol. 48 (Nov. '48), pp. 1032-1048.
[29] Wernham, *TPT*, p. 125, Chap. 16. G. Vol. III, p. 189, 1. 21-23.

the "multitude . . . is guided, as it were, by one mind".[30] Thus laws are taken in some sense or other as the expression of the common mind, or, in Spinoza's idiom, the common will. If there is general lack of obedience to a particular law, it, so to speak, announces itself at variance with the will of the dominion and can no longer be taken as its guide, that is, as a law of the dominion. These points are at bottom compatible with Spinoza's notion of law as issuing from the will of the sovereign only if it is recognized that the ultimate criterion of the validity of a law rests on its acceptance by the multitude subsequent to its promulgation by the sovereign authority. As argued in the next section, not every will of the sovereign is a valid law.

From the above it is clear that the laws which will be disobeyed *en masse* are those which do not appeal to the multitude as advantageous. Nothing is truly a law unless it is tacitly approved by the multitude by virtue of their obedience to it. The true basis of this situation and the important distinction between Spinoza's and Hobbes' notion of absolute sovereignty can be appreciated only after consideration of the notion of natural rights in Chapter II. It can be understood here that law is not anything whatsoever that is claimed by the sovereign to be law without further consideration of whether the subjects recognize the decree as binding. The criteria to determine whether an enactment is a law cannot be purely formal but must include consideration of WHAT the command expresses and whether it is in fact obeyed to a reasonable extent. The enactment may be abortive and not warrant the name law which is reserved for those commands of the state that function as regulative of behavior. The fact that rewards and penalties are required to be attached to the laws does not alter this condition. Spinoza does accept the necessity of adding inducements to the substance of laws insofar as the citizens do not understand the true good of the state and their place in it. Yet he maintains that there are some things, *viz.*, those things against human nature, that the citizens could never be enticed into doing no matter what inducement is offered. If it is attempted to legislate on these matters, the result for Spinoza

---

[30] Elwes, *PT,* p. 301. Chap. 3, Sect. 2. G. Vol. III, pp. 284-285.

will not be a law at all insofar as it does not and cannot attain the requisite obedience. The significance of this condition will be considered in Chapter IV.

F. LAW AS THE WILL OF THE SOVEREIGN

Spinoza's notion of law as a command must be considered with respect to this relation between validity and efficacy. Law is taken as the expressed will of the supreme authority in the commonwealth, a decree stating the desire that certain external acts be done or omitted. If a sovereign issues a particular decree expressing his will, it is not however *ipso facto* a law. "A monarchical dominion... must be ordered so that everything be done by the king's decree only, that is, so that every law be an explicit will of the king, but not every will of the king a law." [31] The will of one man is 'inconstant'; that is, it is not the case that the sovereign always wills that which is best for the dominion and if his decree is sufficiently repugnant to reason and nature, the fact of his desire is not equivalent to the enforcement of the decree. In order for a decree of the supreme authority to be a valid law, in addition to the mechanics of legal procedure, it must appeal to the multitude as an advantageous regulation. The situation is different in an aristocracy in which a council passes laws since in this case there is not the problem of the 'fluctuating and inconstant' will of one man. With a "sufficiently numerous council . . . its every explicit will ought to be law".[32] This dominion is closer to an absolute dominion, that is, dominion held by the whole people. Although an aristocratic dominion is not in fact absolute, it is best if it functions as absolute, which it can do only by eliminating all reasons to fear the multitude. This again requires that the multitude be kept satisfied by being subjected only to laws which they consider advantageous, although they are not explicitly consulted in the passage of particular laws.

In addition, a law can not be at variance with what Spinoza terms 'the foundations' of the dominion, the constitution, written or un-

[31] *PT, op. cit.*, p. 328, Chap. 7, Sect. 1. G. Vol. III, p. 308.
[32] *Ibid.*, p. 347, Chap. 8, Sect. 3. G. Vol. III, p. 325.

written, of the state. These so-called 'eternal decrees' of the sovereign cannot be transgressed or superseded by subsequent decrees, and if this is attempted the subsequent decrees do not count as valid laws. This is not merely the built-in guarantee of a particular constitution or a particular system of common law but is a necessary condition of the stability and permanence of any state. For Spinoza, the sovereign is not above all laws; "It is in no way repugnant to experience for laws to be so firmly fixed that not the king himself can abolish them." [33] Not only is it agreeable with experience but it is necessary for the security of the dominion that the sovereign be subject to the fundamental laws of the commonwealth. Spinoza recognizes here the distinction between laws which are fundamental to the continuance of the form of the state and 'secondary' laws which must be in harmony with them. The fundamental laws cannot be anything the sovereign chooses; they also are subject to ratification by active obedience on the part of the citizens. The fundamental laws, for example, the constitution, are, as it were, the form of life of the state, and must, if the state is to have stability, be firmly rooted in the customs of the people. The particular laws, while they are dependent on the will of the sovereign, cannot be the product of an arbitrary will. The sovereign does theoretically have the position to institute whatever he pleases as law but it is inevitable that certain consequences will follow, the most important being the destruction of the state and of the sovereignty if it is attempted to institute iniquitous laws or laws contrary to the fundamental laws. This theoretic ability is, of necessity, limited in actual practice by the needs and demands of the state.

Thus for Spinoza we do not have the simple equation of law with the command of the sovereign in the sense of law being anything which the sovereign orders. At the same time the law of the state need not be issued by each sovereign in succession. Spinoza speaks of fundamental laws which are 'eternal', that is, they are regulations which are in force throughout successions of sovereigns. Since these fundamental laws define the structure of a commonwealth, they ought to be accepted and enforced in turn by each sovereign in

---

[33] *PT, op. cit.*, p. 327, Chap. 7, Sect. 1. G. Vol. III, p. 307.

order to maintain the stability of the dominion.

The sovereign, in addition to laying down the law, is the sole interpreter of its meaning and application. Were it left to the individual citizen to interpret the law this would be tantamount to allowing him to make law since he could interpret the words according to his own will and purpose. It is also, and for the same reason, the duty of the sovereign to appoint jurists as his representatives to administer the law.

G. INTERNATIONAL LAW

With respect to laws of war and peace, that is, laws governing relations between states, the situation is not one of an acknowledged sovereign commanding his subjects. Commonwealths are independent of each other, in a "state of nature", prior to entering into legal agreement or contract. "Laws of war are the concern of each individual commonwealth only, but laws of peace are the concern not of one individual commonwealth but of at least two." [34] The only connections, legal or otherwise, between commonwealths are peace treaties which are entered into from 'hope of gain or fear of hurt'. According to Spinoza, when the motive for having entered into a contract no longer exists, the commonwealth has the right to break the contract since each commonwealth must consult its own interests and act according to them. Yet to hold that a contract is valid only insofar as the will lasts is to say that the contract is not binding at all. The state which was second party to the contract ought not to accuse the commonwealth which broke the contract of bad faith. A state should understand from the outset that a contract is valid only so long as it is to the advantage of each to subject themselves to its conditions. Since the contract between states has no other force behind it than the will of the contracting commonwealths, it is, on Spinoza's principles, a misunderstanding of the nature of the state to suppose it to remain bound by an agreement when circumstances are changed. The notion that treaties are bind-

---

[34] *PT,* Chap. 3, Sect. 13. G. Vol. III, p. 290, 1. 7-8. Original translation.

ing only insofar as relevant conditions remain constant was introduced into international law by Gentili near the end of the 16th century. It was known as the *clausula rebus sic stantibus,* and originated in canon law, having a private province.[35]

The law of war and peace, or international law as it was designated by Grotius, is rooted in that fundamental law of human nature which disallows men from choosing or remaining in a situation which they do not find to their advantage. Since in Spinoza's time there was no developed notion of a legal code which embraced all nations and to which all had acknowledged allegiance, he did not consider that the breaking of an agreement was an act of injustice or disobedience but rather an inevitable consequence at the moment when advantage had ceased. In fact, each state has the duty to consider the good of its citizens as more compelling than any international agreement. This conclusion does not deny the possibility or value of international law, but is rather, given Spinoza's principles, a realistic appraisal of its foundations and limits. If Spinoza had conceived of nations as related in an international community rather than as independent states at war with each other, it is likely the he would have been more amenable to the notion of the supreme binding power of international agreements. Spinoza appears to disregard the existence of peaceful relations not based on treaties and also of customary practices between nations, as, for example, the recognition of permanent foreign legations. His conception of the international community as composed of independent units did not lend itself to the recognition of such non-legal practices. The treaty, as the sole basis of international understanding would not tend to introduce the trust requisite for extra-legal communication.[36]

---

[35] Arthur Nussbaum, *A Concise History of the Law of Nations* (New York, Macmillan Company, 1954), pp. 94-96.

[36] With respect to the present circumstances of nuclear threat it is of interest to note in the policy of statesmen an increasingly explicit recognition of two possible solutions to an international crisis; either legal control and inspection of weapons or an actual structuring of the situation which guarantees no advantage to aggressive policy, e.g., counterforce tactics. It is this latter point which is reminiscent of Spinoza's insistence that in the final analysis national advantage is the determining factor in policy rather than a supposed sanctity of treaties or a supposed obligation to the international community.

H. LAW AS A MEANS OF THE STATE

The definition of law as 'a plan of living which serves only to render life and the state secure', includes international as well as domestic law. The largest autonomous unit Spinoza conceives is the state and it is for the good of the state that everything must be ordered. The state is not however an abstract self-subsistent entity but the organization of individuals who maintain allegiance to it. The powers of the state are the sum of the powers of its citizens. It has been noted that law is both an instrument which the state uses to control and guide its citizens and an agency which helps compose the actual life and structure of that state. Although law is both the form and the instrumentality of the state, law, or control, *per se* cannot be the end of the state. It will always be necessary for law as a means of the state to subject the substance of its commands to whatever is necessary for men to live in harmony with one another. The state itself becomes a means to the achievement of the welfare of the individual citizens; if it does not fulfill this requirement it instigates its own collapse. Wholesale disobedience to its laws are an index to the malfunctioning of a state with reference to this task of satisfying its citizens. When disobedience reaches a certain point, it is no longer possible to speak of the continuing in existence of the original state. A new form of the state is instituted; that is, a new legal structure, promulgated and enforced by the dissenters. Spinoza does not identify the state with its legal system yet he recognizes that the laws of the state define its character and its tenure, although it is nonetheless true that the state has other functions besides its legislative duties.

At the same time the desires and passions of individual men must be subdued and brought into cooperation with the interests of their fellow-citizens. The function of the state is not to persuade or threaten its citizens to obey its law but rather to achieve for the citizens a way of life which will minimize the conflicts between them and bring each to his fullest development. In actual fact, however, the state is dealing with men who have not, for the most part, achieved the level of full rationality and self-determination. Thus law must approach these individuals on the level of desires and passions, whose instrumentality is reward and punishment, rather than the level of reason. It is for Spinoza an indubitable truth of human nature that men who have achieved only partial rationality must be appealed to on that level and he has no patience with political theories which speak of men being led by benevolent and rational motives. Not only are such theories intellectually false but they lead in practice to abortive attempts at ruling nations. Men can only be appealed to on the level on which they are if the appeal is to be more than empty words.

Given men as they are, the state must make it to the advantage of each individual to obey its dictates and at the same time the laws must be such that actual obedience will be conducive to the security and wellbeing of the state. Spinoza holds that it will always be the case that obedience to the laws of the state is to a man's advantage since without the existence of the state men are in constant conflict and thus unable to achieve those conditions necessary for their preservation and security. This is not to say that each state is in each case the best it can be in all respects, but only that any state is better than no state, any laws better than no laws.

Typically human life is not supportable in a totally unordered condition. For Spinoza this is a truth of human nature and an explanation of the origin function and continuance of the state. The important question for political theory is not to justify the existence of the state as if it were something unnatural and imposed without rationale, but rather to determine the best type of state. Whether the state is good or bad, however, its citizens can never possess a legal right to disobey the supreme authority, although the actual authority of any sovereign is, by natural necessity, limited in scope. The different question of the natural right of the citizen with respect to the sovereign and of the sovereign with respect to the citizen will be taken up below.

It is not necessary for Spinoza to rely on the fiction of an original contract to explain the existence and the rights of the state. Men enter into that social organization only because they understand it to be to their advantage; and they remain subjects of the state from the same understanding. If they did not so feel, no original contract or promise could bind them to obedience because men are simply incapable of doing that which does not appeal to them as advantageous. Of course it can be said that men could be brought to appreciate the advantageousness of keeping a promise — which seems to have been Machiavelli's point — but this simply extends rather than proves the argument. The advantage gained from keeping a promise is referable to one's reputation as a member of a state, and if the value of that membership is what is in question, the end is incommensurate with the means.

Thus if it is taken to be to one's gain to disobey the laws of the state at the risk of its destruction, this act does not violate an original pact but is rather the inevitable response to the actual foundation of the state. A succesful rebellion shifts the power and right of sovereignty and thereby institutes its new law. The fact that Spinoza does not advocate rebellion is, it would seem, for different reasons than that it is unjustifiable. The chaos wrought in a social community by the destruction of its legal and power structure is in most cases not met by gain in the change of government. The causes or conditions of discontent will still be present notwithstanding the fact that a new government is instituted. It is the causes of discontent that must be treated and this can be done as well by the existing government once the dangers consequent on the dissatisfaction of the people are articulated.

Perhaps it can be said that for Spinoza it is the state, composed of the ruler and subjects, which is supreme rather than the ruler or sovereign (except of course where the entire people hold sovereignty). Law then, as intrinsic to the nature and functioning of the state, is the expression and repository of this supremacy and in this posture is superior to subjects and sovereign alike. Given this formula, the impossibility of compelling men to do what is against their desire can be understood since it would be tantamount to the state, that is, the sovereign and the citizens, compelling themselves. In Spinoza's discussion, as reviewed above, there are of course other and more fundamental reasons why such compulsion is impossible. However it can be seen here that the final force behind the laws is the will of the people who are, on any stand, incapable of willing that which is against their will. Although this force may be, and often is, centralized in a so-called non-representative government, law will not achieve the requisite efficacy to validate itself if it does not account for the will of the people.

II

THE NATURAL DIVINE LAW; THE NATURAL LAW; NATURAL RIGHT; AND CEREMONIAL LAW IN SPINOZA

A. THE NATURAL DIVINE LAW

Of particular interest in analyzing Spinoza's conception of the natural Divine Law is the equivocal nature of its claim to be law. This relates to Spinoza's notion of law in general. What is indicated here is the necessity of a re-evaluation of the classical notion of the relation of human law to Divine Law.[1]

By natural Divine law Spinoza refers to "the universal laws of nature, according to which all things exist and are determined ... which always involve eternal truth and necessity".[2] All law is a plan of living but the object and aim of Divine law differs from that of human law. "By divine law I mean one whose sole object is the supreme good, i.e., true knowledge and love of God."[3] The natural Divine law in this formulation is applicable only to men insofar as men are the sole beings of whom it is possible to predicate knowledge and love of God. In its widest formulation the natural Divine law refers to the order and events of nature.

The natural Divine law is a law. — "The word law, taken in the abstract, means that by which each individual, or all things, or some things of a particular species, act in one and the same certain and definite manner, which manner depends either on natural necessity or human decree."[4] To call these eternal truths of God laws, is

---

[1] For a discussion of the natural law tradition, cf. Appendix A.
[2] Elwes, *TPT*, p. 44, Chap. 3. G. Vol. III, p. 46.
[3] Wernham, *TPT*, p. 71, Chap. 4. G. Vol. III, p. 59, 1. 25-26.
[4] *TPT*, Chap. 4. G. Vol. III, p. 57, 1. 23-27. Original translation.

to point to the uniformity and predictability of the operations of nature, the uniformity of behavior which here is taken to be characteristic of law in general.

Natural Divine law is a law in the sense that it determines nature to operate in a fixed and uniform manner. This focus on the aspect of regulation, law as an instrument which regulates behavior, has been historically the most widely accepted characterization of law. It is partially responsible for the notion of human law as carrying some sort of NATURAL necessity, and for the characterization of laws of nature as forces or powers which regulate the process of nature. Spinoza himself makes neither of these mistakes.

The natural Divine law is not a law. — This similarity however between law in general and the laws of God is not adequate to recommend the use of the term law. For Spinoza the conception of God as a lawgiver who can be obeyed or disobeyed is a misleading and dangerous notion insofar as it leads the mind from a correct understanding of God's true relation with the universe. Nothing is free to disobey the laws of the divine will; they are not ordinances which can be obeyed or disobeyed, "followed by gain or loss", but depend "necessarily on the nature of the act performed".[5] "A law which depends on natural necessity is one which necessarily follows from the nature or from the definition of the thing in question,"[6] that is, from the essence of the thing as related to God. Whatever occurs in the universe according to God's understanding, occurs by absolute natural necessity, including the behavior of men as part of the natural universe. The natural Divine law relates to and coincides with this determinate way of existing and acting.

The natural Divine law can not be taken to be a law, nor God a lawgiver in the sense of law as a command which can be obeyed or disobeyed. Natural Divine law relates, in its widest formulation, to natural phenomena, to occurrences which happen by necessity. It can be called a law in the sense of command only by analogy since "God's affirmations and negations always involve eternal neces-

---

[5] Elwes, *TPT*, p. 63, Chap. 4. G. Vol. III, p. 63.
[6] *Ibid.*, p. 57, Chap. 4. G. Vol. III, p. 57.

sity or truth."[7] Spinoza contends that it is only through lack of knowledge, or in deference to the lack of knowledge in an audience, that we speak of these eternal truths of God as laws and of God as a lawgiver who is described as a king or ruler, and as just and merciful "although all such characteristics belong to human nature only, and must be eliminated completely from our conception of the divine nature".[8]

Since for Spinoza the will and the understanding of God are identical, to say that God wills something is to say that he has understood it, which understanding involves eternal truth and necessity. God's will refers only to what exists of necessity, that is, to the structure and events of the natural universe, the order of nature itself. God does not promulgate laws in the sense of commanding what is to take place. His so-called laws embody conditions of natural existence; they are manifestations of God's nature itself. "The operations of nature follow from the essence of God, and ... the laws of nature are eternal decrees and volitions of God."[9] For Spinoza, the laws of God or the natural Divine law comprise the laws governing nature which are eternal and inviolable, although it is only by analogy that it is possible to speak of nature obeying laws.[10]

The natural Divine law teaches perfection. — Spinoza derives the natural Divine law applicable to man from human nature and holds that it, of necessity, is "universal or common to all men".[11] The highest good for man with which natural Divine law is concerned is his intellectual perfection which depends strictly on knowledge of God. "Firstly, because without God nothing can exist or be conceived; secondly, because so long as we have no clear and distinct idea of God we are able to be in doubt concerning all things."[12]

---

[7] Wernham, *TPT,* p. 77, Chap. 4. G. Vol. III, p. 63, 1. 10-12.
[8] *TPT, op. cit.,* p. 79, Chap. 4. G. Vol. III, p. 64, 1. 13-14.
[9] Elwes, *TPT,* p. 86, Chap. 6. G. Vol. III, p. 85.
[10] An event or occasion cannot strictly speaking be said to be ruled by laws as the so-called law is simply the functioning or characteristics of the thing itself. The further analysis of natural law will be developed below.
[11] *TPT, op. cit.,* p. 61, Chap. 4. G. Vol. III, p. 61.
[12] *TPT,* Chap. 4. G. Vol. III, pp. 59-60, 11. 35-1. Original translation.

The decrees of God are concerned with the manner in which men may achieve intellectual perfection or the knowledge and love of God. Any plan of life which leads to this end is called the law of God. The law is held to be intrinsic to all men and governs all their actions on whatever level of achievement they have reached. "We have so intimately deduced it from human nature that it must be esteemed innate, and, as it were, ingrained in the human mind."[13]

"The sum and chief precept . . . of the Divine law is to love God as the highest good . . . not from fear of any pains and penalties, or from the love of any other object in which we desire to take pleasure."[14] Since the love of God is understood to be the final end of all human actions, the natural Divine law refers to the fact that all the actions of men must ultimately be directed to this end if they are to achieve perfection. As indicated, it is not adequate simply to love God as the highest good but one must love him as an end in itself, as the final object of striving. With respect to the natural Divine law, one must achieve a certain development of reason in order to appreciate God as the highest good, a position not gained by the majority of men who for the most part appear to regard the pleasures of the appetites as the chief good. These men, according to Spinoza, cannot be said to live according to the natural Divine law even if they should attempt to love God from fear of the consequences of not so doing or from hope of the reward of their 'faith'. This, for Spinoza, can never be the way to a true love of God.[15] At this point it can be noted that the natural Divine law cannot function, as civil law does, by the persuasion of threats and promises. The law of God must appeal to men directly as expressive of the highest good and as coincident with the ultimate aim of their actions.

[13] Elwes, *TPT*, p. 69, Chap. 5. G. Vol. III, p. 69.
[14] *Ibid.*, p. 60, Chap. 4. G. Vol. III, p. 60.
[15] There appears to be a certain ambivalence concerning Spinoza's notion of the necessity of Divine law insofar as it is possible to make sense of, and he himself recognizes, the fact that men do regard other things, e.g., happiness, as the supreme good, and do act according to their conception. If it is recognized that the Divine law is not a command which orders men to love God as the highest good, but is rather a truth concerning human nature, *viz.*, the fact that the love of God is their highest good, it can be understood that the Divine law does in fact hold with absolute necessity.

In the discussion of Scripture, Spinoza states that the 'cardinal precept' of the natural Divine law is "to love God above all things, and one's neighbor as one's self".[16] This formulation of the law introduces the issue of one's relation with other men as an aspect of the ultimate end of human acts. It is here noted with reference to God's laws that "the true way of life consists, not in ceremonies, but in charity; and a true heart",[17] which again appears to direct the natural Divine law to social considerations. Although these formulations are verbally at variance with that which refers only to the love of God as the highest good, they can be understood as stating the consequences of this one fundamental precept rather than as introducing a totally new content into the law. Spinoza recognizes that one who lives according to reason, that is, one who understands his highest good is to love God, will desire for others the good he seeks for himself. "The good which everyone who follows after virtue seeks for himself he will desire for other men; and his desire on their behalf will be greater in proportion as he has a greater knowledge of God."[18]

B. THE LAW OF THE PROPHETS OR THE CEREMONIAL LAW

Spinoza's notion of the ceremonial law shares certain characteristics of the natural Divine law and of positive law. Although its origin is rooted in a supposed Divine revelation, it shares enough significant characteristics of civil law to serve as an indication of Spinoza's understanding of the interrelation of those characteristics — an analogy which can be of use inasmuch as Spinoza did not gather together his points regarding civil law. The analysis of the law of the prophets will be limited to those aspects which are conceivably analogous to civil law since a full discussion would lead too far into peripheral analysis of Spinoza's conception of prophetic insight, divine revelation and the religious dimension in general.

---

[16] *TPT, op. cit.,* p. 172, Chap. 12. G. Vol. III, p. 165.
[17] *Ibid.,* p. 169, Chap. 12. G. Vol. III, p. 162.
[18] *E, op. cit.,* Part 4, Prop. 37. G. Vol. II, p. 235.

The ceremonial law is positive Divine law. — The Divine law, which is called "indifferently God's Law and God's Word" refers also to "the command of any prophet, in so far as he had perceived it by his peculiar faculty or prophetic gift, and not by the natural light of reason".[19] Spinoza explains that this extension of the denotation of the term is rooted in the fact that the prophets generally conceived of God as a lawgiver so that insights revealed to them by God would be considered as laws of God. The implication here is that this use of the notion of the Divine law is held by Spinoza to be of secondary importance insofar as he dislikes the connotations associated with the anthropomorphic notion of God as a legislator. It is further indicated that the law revealed to the prophets may have a different aim from that law designated the natural Divine law which is common to all men. Spinoza uses the term human laws, i.e., moral and civil laws, to refer to those laws which have a different aim from the natural Divine law "unless they have been ratified by revelation, for in this respect also things are referred to God ... and in this sense the law of Moses, although it was not universal ... may yet be called a law of God or Divine law, inasmuch as we believe it was ratified by prophetic insight".[20] The laws of the prophets which have limited applicability to a given people in particular circumstances will be designated positive Divine law as distinguished from the natural Divine law which applies universally to all men.

From one point of view it is feasible to include the positive Divine law as part of the natural Divine law since the laws of the prophets or the ceremonial law comes to men as a revelation from God. However the differences between the ceremonial law and the natural Divine law are more fundamental. The ceremonial law is adopted to a particular state and a particular people; it is held to be applicable only within a restricted sphere and within this sphere it can be disobeyed. Further the aim and reward of the ceremonial law is of a very different nature from that of the universal Divine law; the latter aims at blessedness or the perfection of men, whereas the former is concerned with temporal benefits and rewards, the temporal prosperity of a particular kingdom.

[19] *TPT, op. cit.,* p. 169, Chap. 12. G. Vol. III, p. 169.
[20] *TPT, op. cit.,* p. 61, Chap. 4. G. Vol. III, p. 61.

The ceremonial law is law proper. — The commands of the ceremonial law, for example, the Mosaic law of the Old Testament, are issued by a prophet in his role as lawgiver and not as a moral or religious authority or leader. "Thus even his prohibition of adultery is aimed at the welfare of the community and state alone; for had he wished to teach a moral precept, aimed not merely at the welfare of the community but at the peace of mind and true blessedness of the individual, he would condemn not only the outward act but also the actual volition."[21] The ceremonial law is instituted, according to Spinoza, with the specific aim of preserving the temporal kingdom, inasmuch as men have need of laws to restrain their desires; it is not concerned with the moral or spiritual condition of the people.

The precepts of the ceremonial law refer to those aspects of men's public behavior which are related to the maintenance of society. "This, then, was the object of the ceremonial law, that men should do nothing of their own free will, but should always act under external authority, and should continually confess by their actions and thoughts that they were not their own masters, but were entirely under the control of others."[22] The ceremonial law functions, as does civil law, to control men's behavior through coercive means and thus works through the persuasion of rewards and threats. Since the ceremonial law is couched in terms of the beliefs of an accepted religion and promulgated by a prophet believed to be the spokesman of God, it is more easily obeyed from devotion than from fear, which, according to Spinoza, is the preferable mode of influence.

The ceremonies instituted by this law are "actions which are indifferent in themselves and are called good only by convention, or symbolize some good necessary for salvation".[23] Thus for Spinoza they can have nothing to do with natural necessity or moral blessedness and are laws only because and so long as they are instituted by command to a people. If the particular kingdom is destroyed, the people are no longer bound to obey the ceremonial laws since

---

[21] Wernham, *TPT*, p. 91, Chap. 5. G. Vol. III, p. 70, 1. 26-31.
[22] Elwes, *TPT*, p. 76, Chap. 5. G. Vol. III, p. 76.
[23] Wernham, *TPT*, p. 75, Chap. 4. G. Vol. III, p. 62, l. 6-8.

these laws have a particular rather than a universal jurisdiction. "As though God had said that, after the desolation of the city, He would require nothing special from the Jews beyond the natural law by which all men are bound."[24] Regarding its sphere of jurisdiction, the ceremonial law is seen to be closer to the civil law than to the natural Divine law insofar as the ceremonial and civil laws do not deal with those things which are directly determined by natural necessity.

C. THE NATURAL LAW

Spinoza's notion of the natural law, markedly different from the classical conception,[25] has characteristics which are of central importance in determining its relation to moral and civil law. The analysis here and in Chapter IV will attempt to demonstrate that the universal immutable character of the natural law makes it, on the one hand, inapplicable as a SOURCE of the particular precepts of civil law, and on the other hand, necessitates its applicability as the CONDITION of the validity of civil law.

The Natural law is a law of God. — The third and final reference of the expression 'God's law' occurs where it is "used metaphorically for the order of nature and destiny . . . especially for such parts of such order as were foreseen by the prophets, for the prophets did not perceive future events as the result of natural causes, but as fiats and decrees of God".[26] Since the order of nature is taken to be identical with the law of God, "the laws of nature are eternal decrees and volitions of God",[27] the metaphorical aspect must refer to the notion of God issuing decrees which can be obeyed or disobeyed, and to the notion that natural events obey laws. This is the only meaning of laws of nature or natural law in Spinoza's philosophy; there is no law intrinsic to nature that is not the law of God, since God is taken as co-extensive with nature. It occurs then that the natural law is eternal, immutable and universally applicable; it is

---

[24] Elwes, *TPT,* p. 72, Chap. 5. G. Vol. III, p. 72.
[25] For a discussion of the natural law tradition, cf. Appendix A.
[26] *TPT, op. cit.,* p. 169, Chap. 12. G. Vol. III, p. 162.
[27] *Ibid.,* p. 86, Chap. 6. G. Vol. III, p. 85.

impossible to speak of events or behavior as obeying or not obeying the natural law. Rather this law is the actual nature of the entity itself, the actual order of the occasion, which entity and occasion are manifestations of God's nature.

There is a natural law of man. — There are natural laws which are specifically related to the nature and behavior of men as distinct from everything else in the universe. If this were not the case, if men were without laws characterizing their behavior, they would be impotent and unable to act since natural laws characterize the determinateness of natural existence. The natural laws specific to human beings, which relate to the essential nature of man, apply universally to all men. They cannot be products of human decree which varies with circumstance, nor can they be altered by human intervention. It is not only the characteristics of man's physical existence which are embodied in laws of nature, but also, and uniquely, his spiritual activities such as thinking, willing and desiring. The natural laws relevant to man comprise those conditions characterizing all aspects of human existence which are amenable to the determination of regularity.[28]

These eternal laws need not necessarily be known to an individual man in order for them to function as regulative of his behavior; nor need they, if known, appeal to him as something desirable or advantageous. That is, the natural law does not require a man's assistance or ratification in order to be determinative of his behavior because the force of the law is derived, not from a man's agreement, but rather from God's ordering of the natural world of which man is part. Since these laws embody the conditions of human existence they are not amenable to change through human agency; men must act in the manner designated by the natural law if they are to act at all. God's law can be neither disobeyed nor altered any more than the nature of the universe can be disobeyed or altered.

---

[28] A man who acts according to the dictates of passion can be said to act against the moral law which states that one ought to act according to the dictates of reason; but he cannot be said to act against the natural law which states that men necessarily seek their own advantage according to their own conception of profit.

D. HUMAN LAWS

Human laws depend directly on human decree. — God cannot directly issue any laws which are in practice actually disobeyed or are capable of being disobeyed. All laws of this type must depend directly on human decree, although ultimately they must be within the possibilities outlined by universal natural laws which relate to occurrences in the natural universe. Spinoza gives two reasons for contending that certain laws, *viz.*, those which are not universal, necessary and unbreakable, depend on human decree; firstly, "the sanction of such laws may very well be said to depend on man's decree, for it principally depends on the power of the human mind",[29] and secondly, "because we ought to define and explain things by their proximate causes".[30] It is clear that God does not give these commands directly to men since if laws are given directly by God it is impossible for men to disobey them. These laws are dependent rather on human agency in the sense that if men do not promulgate them, they are not to be found as laws. This distinction is expressed by Spinoza: "And thus man can, indeed, act contrarily to the decrees of God, so far as they have been written like laws in the minds of ourselves or the prophets, but against that eternal decree of God, which is written in universal nature, and has regard to the course of nature as a whole, he can do nothing."[31]

Human laws are indirectly dependent on laws of God. — The class of laws which are dependent on human decree includes the laws of the moral and civil orders, and the ceremonial law discussed above. Moral and civil laws are neither universal nor necessary products of human agency and they can be disobeyed and altered. Actual moral and civil laws or codes could always be different from what they are. Yet since men are part of the natural world which is ordered by God, it is true to say that ultimately the moral and civil laws are laws of God insofar as He is responsible for everything that occurs in the universe. However these laws of God require men to

---

[29] *TPT, op. cit.,* p. 57, Chap. 4. G. Vol. III, p. 58.
[30] *TPT,* Chap. 4. G. Vol. III, p. 58, 1. 19-20. Original translation.
[31] Elwes, *PT,* p. 299, Chap. 2, Sect. 22. G. Vol. III, p. 284.

pronounce them and can only be rendered efficacious by the agency of particular men in particular historic circumstances. To say this is to recognize that the natural laws of human existence, God's direct laws, are ultimately at the basis of man-made laws. That is, as has already been recognized regarding civil law, there are certain definite and given conditions under which men can operate and control. These conditions establish predetermined limits to the moral and civil laws which can be introduced. Since man's nature is governed by natural Divine law, the moral and civil laws which he determines must be rooted therein inasmuch as the laws of man's determination are HUMAN laws. Human laws then are ultimately rooted in human nature, which nature comes from God.

Since the nature of civil law was discussed in Chapter I, and that of the moral law will be discussed in Chapter III, it is only the natural law which will be developed here. It can be noted at this point, however, that given an intrinsic connection between the unchangeable natural law and the moral law, one might expect that Spinoza will attempt to make sense of the notion of a true or correct moral law.

E. THE NATURAL LAWS OF HUMAN NATURE

The natural laws of man delimit the sphere of possible civil laws and aid in explicating the manner in which civil laws function as regulative of behavior. Alternately, it could be said with equal justice that the natural law determines certain necessary characteristics of civil law insofar as the natural law embodies certain characteristics of human nature.

The following discussion of natural law[32] will be limited for the most part to the laws of human existence insofar as they are directly relevant to an analysis of human behavior.

There is a *conatus* in man. — The fundamental law of all existence is expressed by Spinoza in general terms in the *Ethics:* "Each thing,

---

[32] By nature Spinoza means God or the totality of reality and the manner in which things exist, their mode of behavior. Ultimately these are held to be the same.

in so far as it is in itself, endeavors to persevere in its being"[33] and goes on to note that "individual things... express in a certain and determinate manner the power of God by which He is and acts".[34] "The effort by which each thing endeavors to persevere in its own being is nothing but the actual essence of the thing itself."[35] The essential nature of man is also expressed by this *conatus in suo esse perseverandi* which is the impulse regulating all that a man does and can do. This *conatus*, as the most comprehensive expression of the natural law, is the spelling out of God's power, the power of nature, as it manifests itself in human nature. Every individual is determined by nature to live and act solely in the manner which he judges to be conducive to his own welfare. The choice of each is the choice of self interest, not because he is uninterested in other things, but because he cannot help referring everything to his own endeavor to persist in existence. This is not a question of correct or incorrect motivation but rather a frank statement of the root of all impulse and action. "Now it is a universal law of human nature that no one ever neglects anything which he judges to be good, except with the hope of gaining a greater good, or from the fear of a greater evil; nor does anyone endure an evil except for the sake of avoiding a greater evil, or gaining a greater good."[36] To designate this a universal law of human nature is to claim that it cannot be disobeyed nor altered, that it is, in point of fact, a fundamental condition underlying human behavior — the rule of human acts rather than something which may be chosen by an individual at will as his guiding principle. Spinoza is not dealing at this point with moral considerations but is simply noting the way in which each man functions of necessity — whether he is good or bad, wise or ignorant.

Although a man can only desire that which appeals to him as advantageous and can only pursue that which he desires, he is not always correct in his judgment, yet he is bound to act according to that judgment. All that men do, in their mental as well as their

---

[33] *E, op. cit.*, Part 3, Prop. 6. G. Vol. II, p. 146.
[34] *Ibid.*, Dem. G. Vol. II, p. 146.
[35] *E, op. cit.*, Part 3, Prop. 7. G. Vol. II, p. 146.
[36] Elwes, *TPT*, p. 203, Chap. 16. G. Vol. III, pp. 191-192.

physical activities, are inevitable reactions to causes as given; choices are not free responses in the sense of being anything at all, but rather responses determined by the natural laws of human nature. It is one thing to attempt to persuade a man that something is not to his advantage and quite another thing to attempt to persuade him not to do something which he considers to his advantage. The latter result is impossible of achievement, not because the man is stubborn but because he is a man.

It is by eternal necessity that each strives to maintain himself in existence and thus the actions of each are by the same necessity directed toward a definite end. The *conatus* of the body is directed toward the perseverence of self-movement, that of the mind toward thought, as well as the means necessary in both cases to attain the end. Spinoza contends that although this impulse or striving begins on the level of passion or appetite, there is implicit in this *conatus* the fullest development of man's faculties, the highest achievement of self-movement and thought. The development of the *conatus* becomes then a striving towards perfection or the fulfillment of one's nature. Spinoza nowhere writes as if he expects many to reach this ultimate good but nonetheless the fundamental principle of explanation for all the strivings of men is the attempt to reach their own perfection.

The fact that there is a definite end to which the *conatus* is directed means on the one hand that there may be a final culmination of striving and endeavor and on the other hand that this striving cannot cease until the end is attained. A man cannot reach the satisfaction of a non-striving condition in whatever way he pleases since satisfaction or peace results from the attainment of a definite development, which position carries with it, its own completion.

The *conatus* is a form of the natural Divine law. — The natural law of man's existence, the *conatus in suo esse perseverandi,* is linked with the natural Divine law, to love God as the highest good. The striving for satisfaction or perfection is, on Spinoza's principles, identical with the striving after God. God or reality is the only 'object' that can satisfy man's striving and his desire for the fullest satisfaction. Spinoza obviously does not mean that men strive to be or become God but rather that they strive to be in a certain relation to Him. Men endeavor ultimately to know truth, to know God and to love Him as the final good or end. This is not to say they are aware that they are striving after this but only that this is the final object of all striving, the only point at which the *conatus* can complete itself. For Spinoza the constant struggle is to know God although the struggle spells itself out in its various stages in many different ways, as, for example, in the desire for sensual gratification. One may never achieve the end nor understand it, yet it is nonetheless HIS end, one which he cannot help working towards, and it of necessity characterizes the process of the struggle.

Neither the natural law nor the Divine law relates that one ought to seek perfection, that one ought to attain to knowledge of God, but rather that men do seek perfection, that men do seek to attain to the knowledge of God. As means to this achievement, men strive after many other things, but, according to Spinoza, they cannot strive after these other things as their final end, although they may perhaps think that they do. It is rather more true to say that they strive after perfection conceived under many different forms, but that they can never reach total satisfaction without attaining the fullest development of their powers, the highest level of self-development.

This is the meaning Spinoza gives to his insistence that the natural Divine law cannot be disobeyed and that it is not a law in the sense of a command. The *conatus* is simply another form of the natural Divine law which embodies the condition of men knowing and loving God as the supreme good, and thus shares similar properties. Neither law can be disobeyed since neither law states what men ought to do, but rather embodies what they do do. From the point of view of the integrity of the law it is immaterial whether men acknowledge its truth; what is essential is that men's behavior coincides with its conditions, and this is, according to Spinoza, inevitable. It is not necessary to remind Spinoza that most men do not understand wherein their true perfection lies, that most do not understand that to know and love God is the highest good; Spinoza is acutely aware of this situation, and has placed it at the basis of his ethical theory.

The above argument can be put briefly as follows: all men strive to persevere in existence; this signifies that men strive for satisfaction or perfection; the only true perfection involves the knowledge and love of God; thus all men seek this relationship with God. At no point is it denied that men might concentrate solely on the means, solely on satisfaction of the lower levels of desire; but it is contended that no man can truly seek this partial satisfaction as his final end, notwithstanding the fact that he might, and often does, think that he does.

The natural law is a condition of human law. — In the analysis of civil law above, it was ascertained that there were basic characteristics of human nature which laws must recognize in order to achieve validity. These 'necessities' of human nature are embodied in the natural law or *conatus* which relates to men's search for what they consider best for themselves. This universal law of human nature must be recognized by, and embodied in, civil law if the latter is to function efficaciously as regulative of behavior. If civil law does not recognize the natural law, its precepts will not be binding for the reason that they cannot be obeyed. This situation in its complexities and consequences is discussed below together with the issue of the relation of the natural law to the moral law which encounters the same restrictions.

The moral and the civil laws are not the most fundamental laws of men's behavior; they are subject to the conditions of the natural law which holds universally, without external enforcement. It is, of course, possible for moral and civil law to disregard the necessary truth of natural and Divine law — to say that human laws are subject to the natural or Divine laws is only to say that certain consequences will inevitably follow if these necessary laws are disregarded, namely the instigation of their own impotence and limitations.

The implications of the natural law which are relevant to civil law are expressed by Spinoza in their many variations throughout his political writings, several only of which will be noted: "In general no one will abide by his promises, unless under the fear of a greater evil, or the hope of a greater good."[37] "No one can honestly promise to forego the right which he has over all things."[38] "Each particular state has the full right of breaking a treaty whenever it wishes."[39] "He who seeks to regulate everything by law is more likely to arouse vices than to reform them."[40] "For were the commonwealth bound by no laws or rules, which removed, the commonwealth were no commonwealth, we should have to regard it not as a natural thing, but as a chimera."[41] "The commonwealth, then ... is bound to preserve the causes of fear and reverence, otherwise it ceases to be a commonwealth."[42] "No one ... can be forced or legislated into a state of blessedness, the means required ... are ... above all, free use of the individual judgment."[43]

F. NATURAL RIGHT

Moral and civil law are intrinsically related to Spinoza's notion of natural right although it itself does not have a moral or even an exclusively human character. The natural right of man is of central importance in determining the limits to the power of the sovereign and thus, derivatively, in determining the kinds of laws that may be successfully promulgated.

Right is identical with power. — The most important and pervasive aspect of the natural law is the principle which holds that right is identical with power. "By the right and law of nature I simply mean the rules of each individual thing's nature, the rules whereby we conceive it as naturally determined to exist and act in a definite way."[44] According to Spinoza, nature has the 'sovereign right' to do whatever is in its power insofar as the power of nature is the

---

[37] *TPT, op. cit.,* p. 203, Chap. 16. G. Vol. III, p. 192.
[38] *Ibid.,* Chap. 16. G. Vol. III, p. 192.
[39] *PT,* Chap. 3, Sect. 14. G. Vol. III, p. 290, 1. 14-15. Original translation.
[40] Elwes, *TPT,* p. 261, Chap. 20. G. Vol. III, p. 243.
[41] Elwes, *PT,* p. 310, Chap. 4, Sect. 4. G. Vol. III, p. 292.
[42] *Ibid.,* p. 311, Chap. 4, Sect. 4. G. Vol. III, p. 293.
[43] Elwes, *TPT,* p. 118, Chap. 7. G. Vol. III, p. 116.
[44] Wernham, *TPT,* p. 125, Chap. 16. G. Vol. III, p. 189, 1. 12-15.

power of God who has right over all things. "But the universal power of nature as a whole is simply the power of all individual things combined; hence each individual thing has a perfect right to do everything it can, in other words, its right extends to the limits of its power."[45] Since the laws of nature comprise the powers of nature whatever is done according to the laws of one's nature is done by natural right. ". . . And since the supreme law of nature is that everything does its utmost to preserve its own condition, and this without regard to anything but itself, everything has a perfect right to do this, i.e. (as I said) to exist and act as nature has determined it to do."[46]

Since men are led more by appetite than by reason, the natural powers of men are limited not by reason but by appetite. However, "man, whether guided by reason or mere desire, does nothing save in accordance with the laws and rules of nature, that is, by natural right".[47] In the way that the wise man has the right to live according to the dictates of reason, the ignorant has the right to follow the dictates of passion. In fact until men have reached a level of developed intellect, their passions are their sole guide in this striving to persevere in existence. Thus whatever an individual can attain in any manner he has the right to take for himself. "The right and ordinance of nature . . . only prohibits such things as no one desires, and no one can attain."[48]

Natural law embodies the inevitable necessity with which an individual chooses what appears to him the greater good and the impossibility of neglecting what he judges to be good. Natural right is simply the right to live according to the natural law of one's existence. As a right it is limited in practice by an individual's power to fulfill his desires. Although it is quite true that in a civil state, as has been noted, one abrogates large areas of power and therefore of right, this is not a denial of the principle but rather an example of it. It will be recalled that a citizen can only obey, i.e., abrogate particular rights, if he understands this to be to his advantage, that

---

[45] *TPT, op. cit.,* p. 125, Chap. 16. G. Vol. III, p. 189, 1. 21-24.
[46] *Ibid.,* p. 125, Chap. 16. G. Vol. III, p. 189, 1. 25-30.
[47] Elwes, *PT,* p. 292, Chap. 2, Sect. 5. G. Vol. III, p. 27.
[48] Elwes, *TPT,* p. 202, Chap. 16. G. Vol. III, p. 190.

is, if he expects to gain from the transfer of rights. However an individual can never totally alienate all his rights or allow them to be confiscated. "No one can ever so utterly transfer to another his power and, consequently, his rights, as to cease to be a man."[49] "The individual retains his own right in many of his actions, which therefore depend on nobody's decision but his own."[50] This situation is responsible for the limitations of the sovereign power of a ruler with respect to his subjects. A ruler can not effectively demand that a subject abrogate certain rights inasmuch as a man cannot alienate certain powers.

This notion of definite powers or rights which cannot be transferred and the correlate notion of the limitations of the sovereign power, point to a fundamental difference between Spinoza and Hobbes. Since right is identical with power, Spinoza's claim that one cannot control the expression of all of an individual's powers short of destroying the humanity of the subject, gives a built-in limit to external authority. For Spinoza it is simply a fact that one cannot cease to be a man, and from this it follows that one cannot cede all one's rights or powers. "With regard to Politics, the difference between Hobbes and me ... consists in this, that I ever preserve the natural right intact so that the Supreme power in a state has no more right over a subject than is proportionate to the power by which it is superior to the subject. This is what always takes place in the state of Nature."[51] From the point of view of the sovereign this is tantamount to stating that there cannot be unlimited absolute sovereignty in the sense of all power and right on one side with complete lack of power and right on the other. The limits to sovereignty are grounded in the natural law which recognizes that a man's powers are identical with his existence as a functioning person; thus one's total powers and rights can cease only at the moment when he ceases to exist. Rights or powers for Spinoza are not so much additional properties or qualities of a man as they are characteristic of his essential nature.

---

[49] *TPT, op. cit.*, p. 214, Chap. 17. G. Vol. III, p. 201.
[50] Wernham, *TPT*, p. 149, Chap. 17. G. Vol. III, p. 201, 1. 30-31.
[51] *Correspondence*, Letter 50 to Mr. Jarig Jelles, 1674. G. Vol. IV, pp. 238-239.

Spinoza's professed difference from Hobbes, quoted above, indicates an important distinction in their understanding of the foundations of power or right. For Spinoza the sovereign receives his legislative power from his subjects to the extent that they obey his laws, whereas for Hobbes the power of the sovereign is not attained through actual performance but from an original covenant which transferred all power to him. This allows a conception of absolute sovereignty which is independent of the subject's appraisal of the sovereign and creates difficulties in dealing with the question of unjust government. In Spinoza's understanding the power of the sovereign, being contingent on its proper use, is real only insofar as his laws are such that his subjects can appreciate them to be to their advantage. Thus ultimately, the sovereign's power is functionally dependent on acceptance of its use, whereas in Hobbes' view, the sovereign's power is simply an inalienable attribute of his position. In Hobbes' view there is no distinction between force and power with respect to the sovereign; in Spinoza's view force must be guided by reason if it is to become power.

Natural right is not a moral right. — Spinoza's notion of natural right is substantially different and must not be confused with the later notion of inalienable rights, either of birth or civil dispensation, associated with the correlate notion of duties of perfect obligation. Spinoza is not indicating rights that should not be ceded or whose transfer should not be required, but powers which cannot be transferred, whatever the threat or promise involved. Again this is not an essentially moral issue nor a question of political integrity — it is simply a fact of human nature, which nature is embodied in eternal and unbreakable laws, ultimately rooted in the natural Divine law.

By nature, men's nature which determines his activities, Spinoza does not refer to reason or the rational faculty of man, as would be the case with classical natural law theorists, but rather to the structure or interplay of both desire and thought, adequate and inadequate ideas. Thus when Spinoza states that man's activity and behavior is ultimately determined by his nature, it is not a claim that men are led by reason and that they should be respected as something created by God as a sort of quasi-divine entity. Spinoza does not root his philosophy in a notion of man as the most important and most nearly divine creation of God, and thereby guarantee rights to the human race. Rather men are taken to be natural creatures on the same level with respect to value or proximity to perfection as any other created beings, determined by laws specific to their own nature which constitute them what they are.

The essence of man is not characterized as something more divine than other natural beings but rather as simply the way in which men behave. This 'way in which men behave' is the natural law of man as a species, and that which is an indestructible condition of their so behaving is that right or power of men which is non-transferable. There is no implication here of the superiority of men nor of a recommended moral propriety which allows rights to man. What is given at this point is simply the notion of a natural necessity which is determinative. It is to the credit of Spinoza's liberated perspective that he abstains from judging this necessity as good or bad. The natural order is not a moral order although it obviously may be and is the condition of moral life. Nature is defined by causality and necessity, and since all that occurs in nature is *ipso facto* natural, all events and behavior are characterized by the same necessity. With this recognition it becomes obvious that one must designate a ground for the moral order different from the natural order if one is to develop a moral theory which deals with judgments of value. It can here be understood that Spinoza cannot derive an ethics from natural law, although one might very well expect that an ethics cannot totally disregard that which determines the universe with inevitable necessity.

III

THE ETHICAL DIMENSION AND THE MORAL LAW IN SPINOZA

Spinoza's conception of the ethical dimension, that is, the scheme he offers to explicate ethical phenomena, will be discussed prior to an analysis of the relation between civil law and moral law.[1] It is held to be unnecessary for the purposes of this analysis to discuss the particular tenets of his ethical theory, the actual precepts which he offers as guides to moral improvement.

A. TWO APPARENT DIFFICULTIES WITH THE NOTION OF A MORAL LAW

The central question is whether a theory of morality is consistent with Spinoza's notion of the universality of natural necessity. If, as Spinoza teaches, everything that occurs takes place by a necessity ultimately grounded in God, if that is, the universe and everything that takes place in it is governed by immutable natural laws, is it possible to make sense of the notion of human volition and choice?

A further problem is involved in Spinoza's contention that the universe is not geared to the good of man or any other finite individuals. For Spinoza, nothing is good or bad in itself; everything is from God and expresses His nature in its own way. "For the perfection of things is to be judged by their nature and power alone; nor are they more or less perfect because they delight or offend the human senses, or because they are beneficial or prejudicial to

---

[1] For the purposes of this discussion I have introduced the term 'the moral law', by which I mean the principles comprising the manner of attaining human perfection as they are expounded in Spinoza's ethical theory.

human nature."[2] It is only presumption and ignorance which allows men to think and act as if their judgment or perspective is an actual account of the true good of the universe. The universe and its constituents are in fact of neutral value, neither good nor bad in themselves. Thus the value judgments that men make cannot be based on criteria of absolute or intrinsic value: "What reason declares to be bad is not bad in relaton to the order and laws of nature as a whole, but only in relation to the laws of our nature in particular."[3]

Neither is it accurate to predicate goodness of God insofar as this establishes a standard of perfection (and therefore of reality) external to or different from God which He would be obliged to consider in his acts as Creator. Either 'God' would mean the same thing as 'good' and then we simply have a word, or goodness would be something added to God's nature, which is, by definition, impossible.

On the one hand the universe in its essence cannot be truly characterized by value predicates and yet at the same time men do judge reality in terms of value relative to themselves. The natural or inevitable conclusion at this point might appear to be that there is no relevance whatever in value judgments as applied to the universe, but to Spinoza this is not inevitable, nor is it his conclusion.

The two difficulties relating to the existence of universal natural laws and the characterization of a universe which is value neutral are systematically interrelated. In a universe which is governed in every detail by universal laws, there is no absolute basis for distinguishing 'good' occurrences from 'bad', or 'good' laws from 'bad', if the universe itself is of neutral value. There is simply law and obedience to law, simply the necessity of God's nature which carries no ethical character. Thus it is not possible to designate anything as intrinsically good or bad. It is as if the entire universe was essentially indifferent, with the recognition that the universe as a whole has no end external to itself. God or Reality is taken as an end in itself and each individual thing in the universe has as a final end its place in the natural system.

[2] *E, op. cit.*, Part I, App. G. Vol. II, p. 83.
[3] Wernham, *PT*, p. 273, Chap. 2, Sect. 8. G. Vol. III, p. 279, 1. 33-36.

Vice is as natural as virtue, badness as natural as goodness. These qualities exist with the same necessity, are determined by given causes which have their necessary determination within the causal nexus. God is responsible for what men term evil as well as for what is termed good, and he himself distributes good and evil without regard to the moral propriety of the dispensation. "Both the beneficial and the injurious ... (are) indiscriminately bestowed on the pious and the impious."[4] The causality of Nature mocks, as it were, man's superimposition of ethical categories on its workings, as if their moralizations could be definitive of the causality of the universe.

B. THE MEANING OF MORALITY

We have however Spinoza's testimony that "the inevitable necessity of things destroys neither divine nor human law".[5] Moral laws are held to coexist with universal natural laws. What meaning then does Spinoza give to the notion of the moral law and to morality which allows this coexistence?

The qualities good and bad do not refer to any intrinsic property or essence of things but are terms whose meaning is relative to man. Spinoza's repeated insistence that by good he understands that which we certainly know is useful to us carries the key to the difficulty. The notions of good and evil are admittedly related to one particular species or class of things in the universe, namely man, who forms concepts or ideals of human perfection. "With regard to good and evil, these terms indicate nothing positive in things, considered in themselves, nor are they anything else than modes of thought, or notions which we form from the comparison of one thing with another."[6] Spinoza goes on here to note that "Since we desire to form for ourselves an idea of man upon which we may look as a model of human nature, it will be of service to us to retain these expressions ... By 'good' therefore, I understand ... everything which we are certain is a means by which we may approach

---

[4] *E, op. cit.*, Part I, App. G. Vol. II, p. 79.
[5] *Correspondence*, Letter 43 (49). G. Vol. IV, p. 222.
[6] *E, op cit.*, Part 4, Preface. G. Vol. II, p. 208.

nearer and nearer to the model of human nature we set before us."[7]

Goodness then, although relative to man, is a standard or pattern which can be applied in value judgments. This model of the ideal perfection of man, the exemplar, is consequent on the 'universal idea' which the mind forms of the type, "for men are in the habit of forming, both of natural as well as artificial objects, universal ideas which they regard as types of things, and which they think Nature has in view".[8] The exemplar cannot be a model external to the individual since the perfection or reality of a thing involves the development of its own powers. Moral perfection is concerned then with the development of a man's existing nature rather than with the pursuit of an alien nature. What is indicated here is that the exemplar abstracts from the individual qua individual and focuses the individual in terms of his value as man related to God or Nature.

Moral theory is concerned with analyzing human nature to determine the way in which an individual can achieve this perfection or fulfillment of his essential nature. Since the goodness of man is identical with this achievement, virtue is defined as the power of effecting that which leads to goodness. Moral theory teaches what the virtuous nature is and the way in which one can attain goodness or perfection.

The human individual is a power operating in the natural world within the context of operation of other finite powers. Each individual entity has the power and right to express and develop itself, limited only by natural possibility and its own impulse or *conatus*. This is as true for a man as it is for a stone insofar as man's nature like all natural things is defined and thereby limited by given powers and his behavior is controlled by natural laws. Although these natural laws operate with universal necessity, they are not alien to the nature of the individual but comprise his essential nature. It is inevitable that a man follows the laws of his own nature, i.e., that he expresses his own nature and not that of another being, and this is precisely what renders him a functioning being and makes his powers actual efficacies.

---
[7] *E, op. cit.*, Part 4, Preface. G. Vol. II, p. 208.
[8] *Ibid.* G. Vol. II, p. 206.

The moral law is concerned with the development of man's natural powers in accordance with the modes of functioning governing human creatures. The perfect man is he who has fully developed his powers (virtues) even though he must do so in accordance with certain fundamental and invariable laws of his nature. "For nothing belongs to the nature of anything except that which follows from the necessity of the nature of the efficient cause, and whatever follows from the necessity of the nature of the efficient cause necessarily happens."[9] Although the more capacities a being develops, the more perfection or reality it has, it is important to recognize that each type of entity has different powers which define its possible development and thus the perfection of each thing will be attained in a different manner. Conversely the perfection of each thing can be reached only by developing its own special powers; "a horse, for instance, would be as much destroyed if it were changed into a man as if it were changed into an insect".[10] Thus the good for man, or that which is most profitable, will be essentially different from the good of any other species. The working out of the ethics is concerned with analyzing the special powers and *conatus* of man in order to determine his highest goodness, that is, his true nature (perfection) and that which is most conducive to achieving it.

C. THE RATIONAL PRINCIPLE AND FREEDOM

The power (potency) of man which expresses his true nature, is intrinsically tied up with his reason.[11] Man, insofar as he is led by reason, determines his own actions, that is, he develops according to his own nature. One who is led by passion is passively determined by forces, either physical forces or emotions, external to his true nature, which indicates impotence rather than power. "Our actions,

---

[9] *E, op. cit.,* Part. 4, Preface. G. Vol. II, p. 208.
[10] *Ibid.* G. Vol. II, p. 208.
[11] Reason is not so much a faculty as simply a name for actual processes of thought. Reason, or knowledge of the second order in Spinoza's classification, is adequate ideas of the properties of things, the formal essence of certain attributes of God.

that is to say, those desires which are determined by man's power or reason, are always good."[12]

The *conatus* or impulse of man is primarily centered in his mind rather than his body, thus the adequate functioning of the mind or reason is taken as his essence insofar as it is the highest achievement or reality of human nature. "The primary foundation of virtue is the preservation of our being according to the guidance of reason."[13] The importance of reason for Spinoza is that it alone can enable a man to achieve knowledge or adequate ideas of his true good or of that which is to his advantage. This knowledge allows him to develop the perspective which keeps him from being led by passions that are biased towards the appearance of goodness in the immediate circumstance. The use of reason is to overcome those emotions which are passive by counteracting them with those emotions which are active. Reason itself is a natural thing and is governed by natural laws.

For Spinoza knowledge both of oneself and other finite things as expressions of God's nature is required for directing man's moral development. One must understand oneself and all things as directed by the necessity of natural law in order to appraise properly the causality determinative of behavior. If it is considered that man is free from the necessity of natural laws, it will be impossible to correctly understand his behavior and the causality underlying his motivation and decisions. When it is understood, for example, that men cannot help but seek that which they desire, it is apparent that the question of morality must focus on WHAT is desired, or to use Spinoza's idiom, which emotions are strongest. If the object of a man's desire is that in which he will find his good and advantage, that is, if the desire derives from reason, which gives correct appraisal of what is good or advantageous, the desire ought to be followed. However it is important to understand that the desire will be followed, whether or not it is a desire for what will actually fulfill a man's *conatus,* unless a contrary and stronger desire is opposed to it. This is a law of human nature which must be recognized if one is to advance towards moral emendation.

[12] *E, op. cit.,* Part 4, App. III. G. Vol. II, p. 266.
[13] *Ibid.,* Prop. 56, Dem. G. Vol. II, p. 251.

True knowledge does in a certain sense allow men to control their emotions; "in so far as the mind understands all things as necessary, so far has it greater power over the emotions, or suffers less from them".[13a] For Spinoza the more one is determined by reason, i.e., understands things as they are, the less he is affected by external things and the more free the individual is taken to be. "And this is why I call a man completely free in so far as he is guided by reason, for then he is determined to action by causes which can be understood adequately through his own nature alone. But he is necessarily determined to action by them."[14] Freedom then as self-determination rather than the indeterminism of uncaused actions is possible only to man among finite creatures insofar as he makes use of reason. Freedom is a freedom from external compulsion, that is, impulses alien to man's essential nature, but not from the necessities of human nature, the laws governing man. These laws comprise the conditions in terms of which men must function, and if annulled, would leave the individual impotent, without the necessary causality which characterizes all power as stemming from God. Thus the man who understands his true good or advantage is able to live according to this. He will live freely in the sense that his *conatus* will be directed to the proper development of his powers (virtue) which renders him more effective and thus better able to achieve fulfillment. For the most part it is the powers of the mind rather than those of the body that are of the highest value to men, both in ruling their own lives and in their relations with other men. "The impotence of man to govern or restrain the emotions I call 'bondage', for a man who is under their control is not his own master . . . so that he is often forced to follow the worse, although he sees the better before him."[15] Although the wise man is stronger and freer than the ignorant, it can never be the case that his reason has absolute control over the emotions or passions. Man, as a finite being, is limited in his powers with respect to the infinite power of nature as derived from God, and therefore he inevitably suffers changes of which he is not the adequate cause.

[13a] *E, op. cit.*, Part. 5, Prop. 6. G. Vol. II, p. 284.
[14] Wernham, *PT,* p. 275, Chap. 2, Sect. 11. G. Vol. III, p. 280, 1. 21-24.
[15] *E, op. cit.*, Part 4, Preface. G. Vol. II, p. 205.

Ultimately the endeavor after knowledge ought to bring one to knowledge of God and of all finite things as related to God as the immanent cause. Knowledge of reality is the knowledge of the different ways in which individual things express God under the form of eternity. It is this knowledge which leads to what Spinoza calls the 'intellectual love of God' which is eternal, being identical with the love which God has towards men. "Our salvation, or blessedness, or freedom consists in a constant and eternal love toward God, or in the love of God toward men."[16] This love of God is not for Spinoza a mystical worship of a transcendent being, but rather an appreciation and knowledge of the 'eternal necessity of himself, of God and of things'. In this relationship the individual no longer suffers passively from external determination as a finite creature, but, as referred to God, attains the fulfillment of his ideal self. Since one who delights in this blessedness achieves the power of mind to restrain his lusts, blessedness is virtue or power itself, rather than being the reward of virtue. Perfection of the virtue or power of the intellect marks the eternal aspect of man's essence as part of God's intellect, which brings the individual himself into eternal relation with God and thus blessedness. "Blessedness is not the reward of virtue but is virtue itself",[17] and thus virtue is as it were its own reward, a good in itself, and not merely a means to the achievement of perfection.

D. THE MORAL LAW AS LAW IMPROPER

By living according to the moral law itself man attains not only blessedness, but the only freedom possible to him, self-determination. It cannot in any proper sense be maintained that one is in bondage to the law or that one is free who obeys his lusts. If 'obedience' to the moral law is taken as a burden, reward for the sacrifice will be expected and 'obedience' to the law will be motivated either by hope of reward or fear of punishment, rather than the knowledge that only the law itself offers true satisfaction. This understanding is the highest achievement of man; it is equivalent to

---

[16] *Ibid.*, Part 5, Prop. 36, Note. G. Vol. II, p. 303.
[17] *E, op. cit.*, Part 5, Prop. 42. G. Vol. II, p. 307.

the recognition that the law is intrinsic to the divine plan of the universe. The moral law which Spinoza describes is taken to be the true analysis of the mode of reaching human perfection; since each aims at perfection, although perhaps with an inadequate understanding of it, it is not as something external imposed on man against his will but rather the truest expression of that which he does desire, that is, blessedness. It is, so to speak, as if each gives himself the law insofar as by its very nature, the law, requiring the development of man's reason, can and must arise from each individual — a man cannot be forced or compelled to understand or to seek his own true perfection. Nor are rewards and punishments relevant in that the highest reward is perfection itself, the greatest punishment, lack of blessedness.

Thus the moral law is not a law in the sense of a command imposed on an individual, equipped with techniques to induce one to obey it. Nor is it a law in the sense that the natural law is a law, that is, by carrying universal necessity in the regulation of behavior. The moral law, in stating the way in which men can achieve the perfection of their natures, their specific virtues, is a necessary truth regarding man, yet its fulfillment is not necessary but only possible. One need not become perfect but if one does it can only be in the manner designated by the moral law. Thus it is left to each individual whether he will fulfill this potential of his given nature although the consequences of not doing so follow by natural necessity. Spinoza holds that it is incorrect to speak of obedience to the moral law as if it were something imposed. The law is the mode of man's self-realization; the law itself gives man his freedom insofar as it teaches him to live by reason alone, which constitutes power and virtue rather than subjection.

E. RELATION TO THE NATURAL DIVINE LAW

The fundamental precept of the natural Divine law, to love God as the highest good, is also the essence of the moral law, if it be noted that 'good' means 'good for man'. Both types of laws have to do with man's blessedness and the manner of its attainment. It is neither surprising nor inappropriate that the moral law should parallel the truth of the natural Divine law but it is required to explain the claim that the natural Divine law cannot be broken whereas the moral law, being a product of human will, does not carry the universal necessity and immutability of the natural Divine law. The true moral law recognizes and incorporates the truth of the Divine law, but the moral law requires the individual human mind to recognize the law as a law before it can be instituted as a law for that individual, that is, the law must be given by a man to himself. As noted above, this recognition does not take place of necessity, that is, it is not part of the natural law of human nature, but is only a possibility dependent on the progress and the history of each individual's consciousness. If the moral law were an external command of an absolute authority, that is, God, it would be identical with the Divine law, not requiring individual recognition in order to constitute it a law. It is as if each individual declares the law to be relevant to himself, and it is a fact that there may be and have been many other candidates claiming position as the moral law. Although for Spinoza there is only one true moral law which reflects God's truth for man, the consciousness of this truth in each individual is not innate, any more than a developed intellect is innate. Intrinsic to the nature of the law itself is the necessity that it be recognized as a law, and there is no natural necessity governing apprehension in each individual man. To say that there is only one true law for man is not necessarily to say that each individual knows this; and if the law is such that it can be said to be followed by an individual only if he qua individual is conscious of it, it follows that there may be individuals who neither know nor, *a fortiori,* live, according to the moral law.

An individual cannot be said to be subject to the natural Divine law. It is a law of human existence which is implanted in the very nature of man. It expresses man's nature and its possible perfection and this is true and therefore relevant to each whether or not a particular individual understands it. The natural Divine law, in other words, regards the truth of man's nature; the moral law regards the actual development of man's powers or virtues. To act rightly one must understand the moral law, the fact of blessedness through reason, insofar as this understanding is the moral law itself. The natural Divine law does not require man's ratification, individually or as a species; it is God's law, promulgated through eternity by decree of the divine will or understanding. It states wherein man's blessedness lies and this is true whether or not a single individual has ever understood it. Perhaps, regarding the moral law, it can be said that when a law is such that a man must give it to himself, he must give it to himself if there is to be a law. This involves Spinoza's recognition that goodness and perfection with which the moral law deals are relative to man, ultimately to man's judgment. However it must be appreciated that although Spinoza does stress this relativity regarding the meaning of the term 'good', once this meaning is understood to be that which is most profitable to man, the content of goodness is not left open or indeterminate but has a definite reference. The content of the true moral law cannot be anything an individual chooses once the meaning of good is determined, but for each to recognize the law at all depends on an individual's determination. The natural Divine law relates to man's special nature and mode of perfection as derivative from God; the moral law relates to the fact that each can achieve the perfection specific to his own nature by becoming conscious of wherein it consists. That the perfection spoken of is the same in both laws simply certifies that Spinoza is discussing the true moral law, that is, the law which relates to man's actual nature, the law which embodies the truth of the natural Divine law concerning man's perfection.

F. KEY TO RELATIONS AMONG MEN

The consequences of the moral law bring the recognition that in fulfilling his own nature, the individual becomes more useful or valuable, i.e., more of a good to his fellow men. And thus each finds that it is more to his advantage to associate with virtuous men or men who have developed the powers accruing to the species. "There is nothing more profitable to man for the preservation of his being and the enjoyment of a rational life than a man who is guided by reason."[18] Reason, in distinction to passion, is the only thing which can bring men into harmony with each other. Individuals who follow their own irrational impulses do not agree with man's rational nature, and tend to breed conflict. "In so far as men are agitated by emotions which are passions can they be contrary to one another",[19] and "so far as men live in conformity with the guidance of reason, in so far only do they always necessarily agree in nature".[20]

Man's good is necessarily a common good, a good which, if shared, increases rather than decreases the benefit of a given individual. "The highest good of those who follow after virtue is common to all, and all may equally enjoy it."[21] It is to one's own advantage that others are rational and that they enter into some form of social association. If there is no progress in moral development beyond the initial phase of living according to unanalyzed passion, it is impossible to achieve any significant harmony among men; and since it is impossible for an individual in conflict with others to achieve his true good or profit, i.e., the development of his powers, there is a preassigned limit to the possibility of full moral improvement. Spinoza does not conceive of the pursuit of goodness as a struggle of each by himself and for himself in isolation from others. Each requires others to be at a rational level, and he himself, as he develops his reason, becomes more useful to the other. Spinoza does not however describe man as a social animal because for him men by nature are not social but self seeking on the level of gratification of passions. It is only through the development of reason that one understands the locus of his true profit and sees this to include, of necessity, association with others who are led by reason. Neither is this an instinct which might be termed social. It is only through reason that one understands his true profit or good, and the development of reason is precisely that, a development.

As self-emendation for Spinoza involves reference from the self to God, it can be understood that whatever brings one closer to this

---

[18] *E, op. cit.*, Part 4, App. No. 9. G. Vol. II, p. 268.
[19] *E, op. cit.*, Part 4, Prop. 34. G. Vol. II, p. 231.
[20] *Ibid.*, Prop. 35. G. Vol. II, p. 232.
[21] *Ibid.*, Prop. 36. G. Vol. II, p. 234.

relation, is helpful and perhaps necessary for its achievement. Social relationship with virtuous men is a necessary condition of man's achievement of the proper relation with God, that is, the perfection of reason in an individual is dependent on his association with rational men. Although each individual can act only in attempted fulfillment of his own *conatus,* when he does understand and act with a view to his own advantage, he will find that a means to the achievement of this is not only association with virtuous men, but the attempt to teach the true way of virtue to imperfect men. This is not to say that the fundamental drive here is not one's own interest; this recognition is merely the spelling out of where those interests lie.

To call all men, on Spinoza's stand, selfish, initiates a false dilemma. The issue is not whether one acts for one's own advantage as he understands it — as men, there is no other choice — but rather in what that action consists. The wise man will be most benevolent although he will be so for his own best interests. To call him both selfish and benevolent merely precipitates a seeming paradox. A man who realizes the divine element in himself is of most use both to himself and to society; his motivation is necesarily self-interest but the self and its fulfillment is extended beyond the initial stage of passion and its gratification to include all men and ultimately God.

The self which is sought in the endeavor for moral improvement is the self which is led by knowledge and love of God, abstracted from the coercion of the appetite. The *conatus* of man is, in the last analysis, grounded in reason — this determines the particular form of the *conatus* as specifically human as distinct from the characteristic impulse of any other entity. The *conatus,* having to do with the preservation of the self, is involved ultimately with the preservation of the real self, or more accurately, with the real power of the self, which in the case of man, is reason. Spinoza recognizes that there are many who do not understand this, being concerned mainly with preservation and continuance on the lower levels of self-development, but the true moral law must recognize this fact of human nature insofar as it must embody man's truest good or advantage. If the *conatus* of man were not directed towards self-preservation but, for example, gratification of sensual desire, the good for man or his truest profit might not be the development of his reason; but then we would not be speaking about man as he actually is.

G. THE SPHERE OF RELEVANCE OF THE MORAL LAW

Although living according to the moral law introduces actual manifestations within the sphere of action and interrelationships among men, the law itself is concerned only with the internal events of the mind. It is obvious that perfection of the mind, entailing full knowledge of the self and all other finite creatures in relation to God, has great effect on the actions and behavior of the individual — and Spinoza does not minimize the importance of this. However the proper sphere of the moral law as a guide to virtue, the moral law *per se,* is the internal development of the individual's mind. Since it is essentially impossible to force a given individual to achieve perfection of intellect, it is essentially impossible to coerce a man into becoming moral. The additional circumstance that the law must be arrived at by the individual himself, *viz.,* that intrinsic to the law is the process of arriving at it, attests to the fact that an individual cannot attain moral virtue through the persuasion of threats and promises. It is true however that anyone can do good acts, i.e., acts which a rational man would perform in given circumstances, but one in so doing, does not *ipso facto* become a good man.

This distinction between the good man and the performance of good acts is of fundamental importance to Spinoza's notion of civil law. It is precisely the job of civil law to induce men to do good acts by commanding such acts and inclining the individual by various means to consider obedience as profitable. Civil law however has nothing to do directly with the moral development of men, that is, with their motivation and their understanding of the correctness of their acts. It is better if men obey from laudable motives, but whether they do or not is outside the jurisdiction of the state's machinery.[22]

[22] These points about civil law will be among those more fully analyzed in Chapter IV.

Having designated the sphere of relevance of the moral law as internal, it is necessary to stress that, on Spinoza's principles, to the extent that men are rational, they are social. This point turns on Spinoza's notion of sociality which is characterized as the mutual strivings of men as thinking beings. The power and ability to think, however inadequately it is developed, is the fundamental factor differentiating a community of men from that of other animals. This is not construed by Spinoza as a recommendation that men form such associations but as a recognition that this is, in the final analysis, the basis of any human association. The recommendation regards rather the endeavor after more adequate thought or more conscious processes of thinking — rational desire rather than blind emotion — insofar as this allows men to form more advantageous relationships, e.g., those characteristic of the civil state. The social condition precedes the civil condition, i.e., a community of men living under laws, and although the transition is natural, it does require a certain development. This development is closely tied up with the advance of thought to the recognition of the advantage of living in an ordered state and thus is closely involved with the development of a more rational understanding. It is true to say that to a limited, although very important, extent, morality is at the basis of the civil state.[23]

The formal basis of Spinoza's ethical theory indicates that morality is grounded in the process of intellectual development, that is, the maximizing of control over the emotions or inadequate ideas. Goodness or perfection is relative to the powers of each thing; with respect to men this involves the ability of each individual to reach the freedom of self-determination. The ideal is not then a superimposed image of an ideal human nature but rather the natural development of what is taken to be the specific powers of human beings, ultimately, of the individual himself.[24] Although the moral ideal is and must be relative to human desire, desire itself is typi-

---

[23] Qualification and elaboration of this statement must await clarification of related points in the next chapter.
[24] This point will achieve great importance in the discussion of the relation between moral and civil law, particularly with respect to the ultimate aims of the latter.

cally human and the relativity is, as it were, simply the expression of man as subject. The ideal is the projected image of natural tendencies in their final development. If the ethics of Spinoza is designated naturalistic, it can with equal truth be designated theistic, in that the nature of man, *viz.*, his powers and abilities, are ultimately derived from God.

H. CERTAIN DIFFICULTIES RECONSIDERED

Spinoza claims that goodness is not an intrinsic property of the natural universe and that man's notion of goodness is relative to his own determination. Objective moral theory is not discounted, however, but can be based on Spinoza's recognition of generic traits of human nature — not in the sense of an already formed inheritance of actual characteristics, but powers or *potentia* unique to the human species. With this understanding of man, value can be referred to the development of the essential nature of man, qua species, rather than to the individuality of each with respect to his idiosyncratic development. Goodness and badness are not relative to men as individuals but to men with respect to their shared nature, and thus achieve meaning as terms which are applicable to men as a class. The true moral law is applicable only to men among all created beings, but yet does hold for all men, although it is certainly true that individuals can and do develop their own notions of morality. From the fact, however, that it is possible to develop many false notions of morality and the moral law, it does not follow that there cannot be one true law which holds for all. What is required is the notion of a generic nature, or, in Spinoza's idiom, common powers.

Spinoza's theory of natural law indicates certain conditions and their consequences which necessarily apply to human beings. It is nonetheless true that each individual has his own unique history, part of which is concerned with the development of reason. Although certain things follow as necessary consequences of given conditions, achievements differ from each other in various ways, including that which is designated their goodness and badness. It is irrelevant to object that men do not have the freedom to choose their development since all that they actually do is determined. Spinoza's ethics does not deal with the impossible task of transcending natural law, but rather with self-determination within the conditions stipulated by the natural law.

There is no logical impossibility involved in applying value judgments to behavior which is governed by laws. An act, although determined by efficient causes, is free insofar as the subject himself initiates the behavior; that is, the act is an actualization of his potency, rather than something imposed on men as passive subjects by external causes. To improvise on Spinoza's example concerning the attitude of a thinking stone; if a stone could think not only would it think it was free but it would judge some stones to be better than others, some ways, for example, of falling, better than others. And it would make sense to consider such notions even though it might be perfectly clear that the stone has no choice at all, for example, in the way in which it falls. What is at stake here is the question of which value predicates to apply to the multiplicity of actions and dispositions with the key lying in one's conception of virtue and vice, power and impotency.

An individual retains integrity and efficacy, that is, virtue, notwithstanding the fact that his behavior is determined by given laws and it is the individual as a functioning being which is judged. He is responsible for himself, although self-determination can be achieved only in certain ways. He is responsible in the sense that as a man he has the possibility of self-determination. A good man will be one who finds pleasure in those things which are truly profitable, although he, as anyone else, will be able to desire only those things which appeal to him as advantageous. The fact that reason is the means by which an individual can learn what is truly profitable signifies that the rational man will be able to act for his true advantage. Men will be more efficient, their natural powers more fully developed, to the extent that their emotions are determined by reason rather than being passively subjected to external forces. Men will always be guided by emotions; the task for ethics is to determine which emotions are more advantageous.

The natural law and the natural Divine law as laws intrinsically rooted in human nature provide the conditions within which the moral law must be developed. The natural law and the Divine law comprise the essence of man, the *conatus* ultimately aimed at perfection and rooted in reason; the moral law focuses the attainment of this perfection through the development of one's powers (virtues), particularly the power of reason. While there is no necessity governing the individual's acceptance of the moral law nor his behaving according to it, it is the case, of necessity, that one cannot be moral or become perfect unless he does so live and act.

Ethical perfection is for Spinoza the most essential and total achievement of human endeavor. For Spinoza as for the classical Greek philosophers all men aim at perfection, which is identical with blessedness, or, in the more secular language of ancient Greece, identical with happiness. To give an adequate account of men, their behavior and relations with other men, it will always be necessary to refer to their inevitable, albeit indirect, striving after perfection. Perhaps it will not be too unusual a surprise if civil law, as a human endeavor, is understood by Spinoza to aim, however indirectly, at the moral perfection of man.

IV

THE RELATION BETWEEN CIVIL LAW AND A HIGHER LAW IN SPINOZA

A. GENERAL CONSIDERATIONS

In Spinoza's understanding the Divine law embodies that which is truly to men's advantage; the natural law embodies the tendency of men to pursue that which they conceive to be to their advantage; and the moral law states that men ought to understand their true advantage and act according to it. Spinoza's conception of the natural law is quite different from the classical notion insofar as there is no moral or evaluative element attached.[1] The law holds with absolute necessity; it is not composed of recommendations imposed on men to which they ought to conform but embodies the natural tendencies of human nature, the conditions implicit in human behavior. The natural law does not guarantee that men always pursue their true advantage but only that which they consider to be their true advantage. Nor does the natural law recommend that men act in this manner; it merely comprises the conative dimension of human nature which is neither good nor bad, but rather valuationally neutral. Virtue, or the power to approach perfection, is a good but the fact of the natural striving is neither good nor bad.

If on analysis it appears that civil law must conform to the natural law this claim would have radically different meaning from the typical natural law claim. There would be no stipulation or guarantee of any ethical principles incorporated in civil law but merely the fact that it allows men to pursue what they conceive to be to their advantage. This coincidence or non-coincidence of civil

---

[1] For a discussion of the Natural Law tradition, cf. Appendix A.

law with natural law would mark the difference between an efficacious and a non-efficacious law[2] but it would not guarantee its material justice. That is, if a civil law commands behavior which does not appeal to the majority as advantageous, the law will not be obeyed, it will not function as regulative of behavior. However it is quite possible for an evil law to appeal to an unenlightened majority as advantageous. Since Spinoza's natural law is significantly different from the classical conception of a natural (moral) law, it cannot be expected that the consequences of the relation between civil law and natural law, if it should occur that there is a necessary relationship, will give the traditional guarantee of material justice.

In further contrast with the natural law tradition, Spinoza makes a clear distinction between the natural law and the moral law. These laws refer to two different spheres of human behavior, the natural law to the necessary, the moral law to the possible and recommended, although there is a definite relation between them. The moral law however is not immutable insofar as it states what OUGHT to be done. If the moral law is taken to be the higher law to which civil law must conform, there is no necessary conformity between civil law and justice or goodness insofar as the moral law does not regulate behavior with necessity.

In short, in contrast to the natural law tradition which claims a natural law that includes moral principles to which civil law must conform, Spinoza's philosophy does not offer a law which is both regulative of the content of civil law and carries ethical import. The immutable natural law is morally neutral and the moral law is not necessarily regulative of behavior. It is possible however, given this scheme, to claim that civil law necessarily conforms to both the natural law and the moral law. To say this is tantamount to saying that only good or just laws are valid laws. Spinoza himself does not make this claim but he does maintain that all valid laws, even if unjust, do ultimately serve a moral purpose with respect to human development. It is contended in this chapter that this point cannot be substantiated within Spinoza's legal theory.

---

[2] This point is argued in Chapter I, Section E.

The argument of the chapter develops as follows: Spinoza's claim that law has a moral end is provisionally substantiated by an analysis of his notion of the FUNCTION of law. The conditions necessary for a law to be valid are analyzed, from which it follows that it is possible for both just and unjust laws to be valid, i.e. law is essentially amoral. However Spinoza notes that civil law cannot have any content whatsoever but must conform to the conditions embodied in the natural law of human beings. This point hinges on the claim that a law, to be valid, must achieve a certain efficacy which is impossible if it attempts to institute behavior counter to fundamental natural tendencies. Since Spinoza's natural law is not a moral law there is no guarantee on this stand that valid laws will achieve justice.

With respect to the necessary agreement of civil law with natural law Spinoza claims that men cannot obey laws which command behavior conceived to be contrary to their advantage. However, law, which is a coercive instrument, can induce men to do that which might in itself be considered disadvantageous as well as evil. This is achieved through the threat of sanctions. Certain behavior however, sufficiently alien to human nature, cannot be commanded in spite of the force of sanctions. Thus there are two classes of evil laws; those which can achieve (through sanctions) the requisite efficacy to be instituted as valid laws, and those which cannot.

It is then argued that Spinoza attempts to justify evil laws by an appeal to their function as part of a valid legal system. The legal system itself is held to be morally justified by an appeal to its function in the state which is taken to be a necessary condition for the achievement of the moral emendation of the individual. Spinoza's belief that the subject has a moral obligation to obey all laws and that the sovereign has a moral duty to promulgate just laws is considered within this framework.

Finally the notion that a legal system achieves a moral significance as a tool of the state is re-evaluated. It is contended that Spinoza's principles allow the possibility of an unjust legal system that has no value either in itself or as a means of helping the state fulfill its moral function; thus particular evil laws cannot be justified on the grounds that they are part of a functioning legal system.

There is then in Spinoza's theory no intrinsic connection between civil law and the achievement of morality; although there is a necessary relation between civil law and natural law this relation does not guarantee material justice, but merely stipulates that there are certain commands which cannot achieve the efficacy necessary to validate them as laws. Thus law cannot be anything whatever that the sovereign commands — there is a large class of possible laws but outside these limits laws cannot be validated. The boundaries are defined not by ethical requirements, but rather by natural necessity.

B. THE END OF CIVIL LAW

The end of law is security. — Spinoza states that the end of civil law is peace, security and the preservation of the state. The common good or "the public welfare is the sovereign law to which all others, Divine[3] and human, should be made to conform".[4] It must be determined whether Spinoza's definition of civil law as a "plan of living which serves only to render life and the state secure,"[5] has packed into it the idea of a necessary relation between civil law and the moral or natural law. Another way of dealing with the same question is to analyze Spinoza's criteria for judging laws as valid (Cf. section C). This analysis inevitably ties up with the notion of the end of law if it is claimed that law does in fact have a given end which is essentially rather than accidentally related to its essence.

Justice is necessary for security. — A necessary condition for rendering life and the state secure is that they must be preserved. However the simple fact of preservation is not sufficient to guarantee security. To achieve security the state must institute a harmony or concord among its members, which harmony must include the rela-

---

[3] Spinoza is referring to POSITIVE Divine law, generally designated the ceremonial law, instituted by human beings for the purpose of achieving security and peace in a temporal dominion.
[4] Elwes, *TPT,* p. 249, Chap. 19. G. Vol. III, p. 232.
[5] *Ibid.,* p. 59, Chap. 4. G. Vol. III, p. 59.

tion of the ruler to his subjects as well as the relation of the subjects to each other. If occasions exist which render dissension and rebellion feasible the state cannot be called secure. "The things which beget concord are those which are related to justice, integrity, and honor; for besides that which is unjust and injurious, men take ill also anything which is esteemed base, or that anyone should despise the received customs of the State." [6]

Spinoza notes that there are two other ways of achieving concord but each of them has limitations: "Concord, moreover, is often produced by fear, but it is without good faith."[7] and, "Men also are conquered by liberality . . . But to assist every one who is needy far surpasses the strength or profit of a private person . . . Besides, the power of any one man is too limited for him to be able to unite every one with himself in friendship."[8] Thus in order for law to fulfill its function, the citizens must be united through justice, integrity and honor. If a law is to achieve its end it must be a means to justice, integrity and honor; it must be a just or a good law, where good refers to the content of the law considered as tied up with material justice. Spinoza's notion of justice, essentially legal justice, is indicated briefly in the *Ethics,* "In a natural state it is impossible to conceive a desire of rendering to each man his own or taking from another that which is his; that is to say, in a natural state there is nothing which can be called just or unjust, but only in a civil state, in which it is decided by universal consent what is one person's and what is another's."[9]

Although law is taken to have a definite moral aim, this does not necessarily entail that a law must fulfill this aim if it is to be a valid law. This hinges on the relation between the standards for good law and the notion of the validity of a law. It must be determined whether there is an implicit identity of law with good law, or law which fulfills the end of civil law, which end on the above analysis, has been shown to be connected with justice.

---

[6] *E, op. cit.,* Part. 4, App., No. XV. G. Vol. II, p. 270.
[7] *Ibid.,* No. XVI. G. Vol. II, p. 270.
[8] *Ibid.,* No. XVII. G. Vol. II, p. 270.
[9] *E, op. cit.,* Part 4, Prop. 37, Note 2. G. Vol. II, pp. 238-239.

C. THE VALIDITY OF A CIVIL LAW

For a law to be a valid law it must, on Spinoza's analysis, fulfill certain definite requirements. It must be a command issued by a sovereign to his own subjects; it must provide a sanction, either a reward or punishment. It is implied, although not explicitly stated by Spinoza that it must in some way or other be known to those who are subject to it, promulgated either in writing or verbally. It is also implied, in his discussion of the necessity of judicial interpretation, that some laws at least must be stated in general terms. All of these requirements are merely formal and do not stipulate any particular content, or guarantee material justice.

Law must attain a certain efficacy. — As noted in Chapter I, Section E, a law must attain a certain efficacy to be valid, that is, it must function to a reasonable extent as regulative of behavior. In determining whether this condition guarantees the presence of a definite ethical content in the law, Spinoza's notion of the status of ethical terms carries the key to the relation between validity and efficacy.

As noted in Chapter III, Section B, Spinoza conceives of ethical and value predicates in general as products of the human mind. From another point of view this is equivalent to saying that the natural law is not a moral law. Value predicates are nonetheless related to human nature although not in any deductive sense derivable from a consideration of the generic traits of human beings. Men believe that those things which they desire are good and they desire that which they consider to be to their advantage. There is an important distinction between that which appears to each as good or advantageous and that which is truly good or advantageous. Only the notion of the true good is relevant to legitimate ethical value judgments. The distinction between the apparent and the true good hinges on Spinoza's analysis of the natural laws of human nature which relate to men's desires and actions (Cf. Chap. II, Sect. E.). Although the natural and ethical aspects of men are of two different orders there is an intrinsic relationship between them. The true good is that which aids an individual in the fullest development of his powers or virtues. Thus for a law to be good it must function as a means to the development of an individual's natural powers, it must be truly to his advantage.

Spinoza's distinction between nature and value is extremely important for a correct understanding of the civil law. If the moral law were the same as the natural law which is immutable, then the moral law would be immutable. If the validity of civil laws is dependent in some way or other on its relation to the natural law, it would follow that all laws must be good. Spinoza holds that the true moral law, although it is one and unchangeable, is distinct from the natural law and need not necessarily be known or followed by an individual man, nor need it necessarily be the sovereign's guide in forming laws.

It is necessary to determine whether a law which does not coincide with the precepts of the moral law can function as regulative of behavior. Only if an unjust law is one which attempts to command behavior contrary to the natural behavior of men would it be ultimately impossible to obey unjust laws. This is equivalent to commanding a person to do something which does not appear to him to be to his advantage.

It is necessary to recall at this point the meaning Spinoza gives to good and bad in the true sense of the terms. Good is defined as "that which we certainly know is useful to us"[10] and evil as "that which we certainly know hinders us from possessing anything that is good".[11] The word 'certainly', referring to true knowledge, renders Spinoza's ethics nonsubjectivistic, which, with respect to the above discussion, means that there are definite things which are, and definite things which are not, to our advantage as men. Thus a bad or evil law will be one which attempts to institute behavior which is actually disadvantageous, i.e., things which lead men away from the development of their natural powers. As to whether a man is capable of desiring and of doing things which hinder or negate his natural development, Spinoza recognizes that men can and often do desire that which is not to their true advantage — not because they do not desire what they conceive to be advantageous but be-

---

[10] *E, op. cit.,* Part 4, Def. 1. G. Vol. II, p. 209.
[11] *Ibid.,* Def. II. G. Vol. II, p. 209.

cause they are often mistaken in their conception. This is the condition of the irrational or impotent man.

An evil law need not necessarily be understood by the citizens to be against their advantage and will not be so understood unless the individuals have a correct notion of their true advantage. That is, except in a state in which the majority of people are rational, i.e., understand and desire their true advantage, it is indeed possible that the majority may obey an evil law, conceiving obedience to the law to be advantageous. Thus an evil law can achieve the efficacy necessary to validate it as part of a legal system. On the other hand, if an unjust law is understood to be antagonistic to one's advantage it will not be obeyed, nor would a just law under the same circumstances. If it is asked whether men as a matter of fact consistently recognize evil laws as disadvantageous, both history and Spinoza's own analysis indicate a negative answer.

Sanctions can act as inducements to obey. — However the situation is a good deal more complex than this. A particular law is not an isolated command but is part of a system that functions coercively. It is necessary to consider the case of obedience to a law which IN ITSELF is recognized as disadvantageous; to consider to what extent sanctions are capable of inducing men to obey commands which would, taken by themselves, be considered contrary to their advantage. Secondly, it must be asked whether it may not as a matter of fact always be to one's advantage in the last analysis to obey the laws of a state, including those recognized as iniquitous, insofar as continuous or habitual disobedience will destroy the state, the existence of which Spinoza takes to be of great and irreplacable value.

With respect to the first point, Spinoza recognizes that sanctions can and do act as significant inducements. It can be readily appreciated that it is often more advantageous to obey certain dictums which one considers to be evil than to suffer the consequences of disobedience, whether they be tangible punishment or loss of reward. However there are certain evil laws that cannot be obeyed however heavily they are sanctioned. This situation ties up with Spinoza's understanding of natural rights or powers, discussed in

Chapter II, Section F, where the point is made that there are certain powers which a man cannot cede short of losing that which characterizes him as a human being. Important examples of these powers or rights are the ability to think, decide, will, worship and believe. If for example, a sovereign attempted to legislate what his subjects must believe, a sanction, even the sanction of death, could not effectively enforce the command. External control of beliefs is simply in the nature of things unachievable, and on principles of Spinoza's moral theory, the attempt is evil. "No one can transfer to another his natural right to reason freely, nor the faculty of judgment, nor can he be compelled to do so."[12]

This guarantees the sanctity of certain natural rights of man, not because they are primarily moral rights, because they are not. Rights have to do with moral value only to the extent that they are tied up with the power of men to achieve their own fulfillment; first they are natural and become infused with moral value when recognized as essential to human development. Evil laws that demand behavior contrary to natural law can function, if sanctioned severely enough, as regulative of behavior, although there are, as noted, some evil laws which can not be enforced. Thus a large class of unjust laws, through the efficiency of sanctions, can achieve the efficacy necessary to render them valid. Since men are often not aware that a given law is to their disadvantage, it is not always necessary to resort to the efficiency of sanctions in order to explain their acceptance of the law.

It is always to one's advantage to obey. — With regard to the second question noted above concerning the ultimate value of a state, this introduces the problem of whether it can ever be to one's advantage to disobey a law at the risk of dissolving the state. History has shown clearly enough that men have often thought it was to their advantage but Spinoza does not give a simple answer here. First it is necessary to note Spinoza's distinction between the state and the form of the state: breach of civil laws amounting to an internal revolution does not destroy the state *per se* but rather the

---

[12] *TPT,* Chap. 20. G. Vol. III, p. 239, 1. 10-12. Original translation.

existing form or (legal) structure of the state. Spinoza contends that it is often to one's advantage to change the legal structure of a state in that men naturally strive to improve their condition. However he is equally as sure that the transfer of power to a new government consequent on revolution is not the best means of achieving improved conditions. The cause of the dissatisfaction must be treated and this requires changes which can as well be done by the existing government if it is made to understand that its continuance in power is contingent on the satisfaction of the citizens. It is not to one's advantage to attempt forcibly to change the governmental system by disobeying its laws. Spinoza is not interested in the power politics of blackmail but rather the most rational and effective solution of the manifest difficulties.

That men do force rebellions does not prove that this is truly to their advantage but merely that they do not as yet understand the proper means of achieving the fulfillment of their desires. "For the man who decides to obey all the commands of the commonwealth, whether through fear of its power, or because he loves tranquillity, is certainly pursuing his own security and advantage in accordance with his own judgment."[13] Spinoza condemns the seeming advantages of rebellion with the intention of promoting an understanding of the proper techniques to bring about improvements, for example, those of the democratic state which keeps its legislation closer to the will of the people. Spinoza does not disapprove of disobedience on the grounds that the state can do no wrong but notes simply that this is not the most efficient means to correct those wrongs. Thus with respect to evil laws (except those which so fundamentally counteract a man's advantage that he is incapable of obeying them), Spinoza holds that men have an absolute duty to obey them and both an obligation and right to discover other means which may bring about their recall.

Evil laws may be valid. — Thus Spinoza's position comes to something like the following: a subject ought to obey a law, whether it is bad or good, unless in fact he is incapable of obeying the law in

---

[13] Wernham, *PT,* p. 287, Chap. 3, sect. 3. G. Vol. III, p. 285, 1. 28-31.

that it demands actions fundamentally antagonistic to his nature. Men are capable of obeying some, although not all, evil laws; that is, there are built in limits to the degree of irrationality or impotence a man can exhibit *qua* human. Outside these limits evil laws can be enforced.

There are then two classes of evil laws; those which cannot under any circumstances be obeyed in spite of being sanctioned (Class I) and those laws which can be obeyed although they are evil (Class II). Laws of Class II can achieve the requisite efficacy to constitute them valid laws whereas laws of Class I cannot become valid laws. Valid evil laws ought to be obeyed until they are superseded by other laws insofar as obedience is necessary for the maintenance of the state's jurisdiction.

Laws have value as part of an efficacious legal system. — There are indications in Spinoza's philosophy that this conclusion is not the final truth; he does not seem to want to allow that laws which fulfill no moral purpose are as close to true laws as are just ones. "I am greatly astonished that the celestial mind was so inflamed with anger that it ordained laws, which always are supposed to promote the honour, well-being, and security of a people, with the purpose of vengeance, for the sake of punishment; SO THAT THE LAWS DO NOT SEEM SO MUCH LAWS — that is, the safeguard of the people — AS PAINS AND PENALTIES."[14]

Spinoza holds strictly to the notion that law has a certain definite aim although laws which do not fulfill this end can be valid laws. What exactly does this mean and is it a contradiction? Must he be interpreted to hold that civil law SHOULD have a definite aim? From consideration of the text, it appears to this writer that we cannot so interpret Spinoza but must take him to be saying that law in its essence does have a certain aim. In attempting to make sense of laws which are valid yet antagonistic to the end of law, a distinction can be made between individual laws and the entire legal structure of which a particular evil law is a part. With respect to the legal code of a state the same necessary conditions of validity hold as

---

[14] Elwes, *TPT,* p. 233, Chap. 17, (my emphasis). G. Vol. III, p. 218.

held for particular laws. Spinoza's position seems to indicate that if the code itself is iniquitous to a significant extent, it cannot achieve the requisite obedience and thus any particular law could not be validated insofar as it could not be enacted and promulgated as part of a legal institution. At the same time that this takes care of the question of non-efficacious legal systems it would appear to supply the answer to the possible contradiction implicit in the notion of a bad law.

For Spinoza, if a law, good or bad, is part of an efficacious, *viz.*, substantially just, legal system, it is taken to serve a definite purpose as a part of that system. Thus even if a particular law is evil it functions, in a wider analysis, in bringing men to their true good insofar as obedience to it strengthens the legal code which is taken to be a good code. Given this intrinsic connection between a particular law and a legal code, an evil law can be seen to fulfill a purpose beyond itself that is a means to human development.

These points amplify Spinoza's insistence on the importance of a legal structure in the state. It seems *prima facie* impossible for a valid system to be totally evil because of the necessity of attaining substantial obedience. Any particular law in a legal system obtains by association, as it were, a certain value, and as part of a valid legal system is taken as a valid law if it has obtained the requisite obedience. In short, although a particular law may itself be evil, i.e., not aim towards aiding the development of men's powers, insofar as it is part of an efficacious legal system, it achieves a certain value. It still remains that not every will of the sovereign is law; the requirement of efficacy, which is related to the content of the law, is the key here; however, there may be evil laws which are both valid, and on the above analysis, justifiable.

Spinoza does not guarantee that all laws in a system will be good laws, that is, there is no guarantee of the material justice of all laws. Yet even evil laws attain a certain value as part of a valid legal system. Since there are certain fundamental natural rights or powers whose exhibition cannot be annulled by legislation, at the extremes there can be said to be a guarantee against injustice.

D. THE DUTY OF THE SUBJECT AND OF THE SOVEREIGN

The subject has a moral duty to obey. — The citizen has an absolute obligation to obey all laws, good as well as bad, except of course those laws which men are, by their nature, incapable of obeying. According to Spinoza it is always to a man's advantage to obey the laws of the state insofar as this retains the power of the state without which there can be no hope or possibility of peace, and in the final analysis, of moral emendation. "That the preservation of a state depends mainly on the loyalty of its subjects, and on their excellence and steadfastness in executing commands, is taught very plainly by both reason and experience."[15]

It could be said that Spinoza recognizes a *de facto* right of revolution, yet at the same time holds that the state is such a great good that disruption of it could never be to anyone's advantage. The state is a prerequisite to moral development, it institutes the conditions necessary for rational emendation. That is, men living in a precivil condition are not in a position where they can develop ethically. Spinoza contends that since the state should be guided as it were by one mind, "What the state decides to be just and good must be held to be so decided by every individual. And so, however iniquitous the subject may think the commonwealth's decisions, he is none the less bound to execute them."[16] There are, as noted above, certain commands which men are not obliged to obey but this is not because the commands are evil but because the men are simply incapable of obeying them.

Since men have an obligation to obey unjust as well as just laws, this would seem to be not a moral obligation but rather a practical or pragmatic one. However if this question of the kind of obligation is considered within the wider framework, it can be seen that there is a definite purpose to obeying all laws, *viz.*, to maintain the security of the state, and this ultimately ties up with the conditions of man's moral emendation. "It is impious, as well as unjust, for a subject to follow his own will and contravene his sovereign's decree, for if this were universally permitted it would inevitably lead to the

---

[15] Wernham, *TPT*, p. 153, Chap. 17. G. Vol. III, p. 203, 1. 12-14.
[16] Elwes, *PT*, pp. 302-303, Chap. 3, sect. 5. G. Vol. III, p. 286.

destruction of the state."[17] If obedience to law is taken as a necessary condition of moral emendation, the fact of obedience achieves value with respect to the moral development of men. The habit of obedience in a subject both strengthens the state and achieves a moral value with respect to the increased worth of the subject as a rational human being. "He cannot even contravene the judgement and dictate of his own reason in carrying out the sovereign's decrees, for it was with the full approval of his own reason that he decided to transfer his right to determine his actions to the sovereign."[18] On this stand then obedience is not morally neutral, not merely practical, but as a necessary condition of full moral emendation, achieves moral value.

To contend that one has a moral obligation to obey an evil law sounds paradoxical if obedience to the law is taken as an end in itself. If understood as a means to a moral end it is certainly possible to be morally obliged to obey an unjust law. It is this writer's belief that it is Spinoza's intention throughout his political and ethical writings to explicate the close connection between the civil and moral dimensions, the fact that civil concord is necessary for the rational life. If so the above interpretation would be closer to Spinoza's understanding of morality at the basis of the civil state than those criticisms of his theory which contend that there is no place for moral obligation in Spinoza's conception of the civil state.

Laws themselves, being commands with sanctions attached, do not operate as moral laws, i.e., laws directly concerned with the moral emendation of the individual, but rather as tools by which the sovereign can demand submission on the part of his subject. This submission applies to bad as well as good laws. "Wherefore, if a man, who is led by reason, has sometimes to do by the commonwealth's order what he knows to be repugnant to reason, that harm is far compensated by the good, which he derives from the existence of a civil state."[19] Once a state is established with reasonable security, the further moral development of the citizens as well as of the

---

[17] Wernham, *TPT,* p. 233, Chap. 20. G. Vol. III, p. 242, 1. 6-9.
[18] *TPT, op. cit.,* p. 233, Chap. 20. G. Vol. III, p. 242, 1. 9-13.
[19] Elwes, *PT,* p. 303, Chap. 3, sect. 6. G. Vol. III, p. 286.

rulers becomes possible. With respect to the laws themselves this means that as tools of the state they gain a moral force and the duty to obey them becomes a moral duty.

Although the sphere of applicability of the moral law is internal while that of the civil law is external, it is quite possible to consider a direct moral obligation to obey civil laws that institute rational conditions in the state which are conducive to moral development. Good or rational laws are morally obligatory on the subjects, although there is no reference here to the motive of the citizen but merely the fact of obedience. With respect to moral development, the motivation of the individual is significant but the sphere of civil law, having only external jurisdiction, cannot be concerned with this. Obedience to evil laws is also the civic responsibility of the citizen; although, as noted above, these laws do not directly aid in moral emendation, they indirectly do so by strengthening the state which is a necessary condition of morality. A preponderance of bad laws will ultimately destroy the power of the state and in so doing announce their own impotence. However until that point of negligible efficacy the citizen has a moral duty to obey evil laws as well as good laws.

The sovereign has a moral duty to promulgate just laws. — It is necessary to consider next the relation of the sovereign or legislator to the civil law; the extent of his responsibility or obligation with respect to the laws he promulgates, and whether he can be said to be subjected, in any sense, to the civil law. It is obvious that a legislator can and does promulgate both good and bad laws, rational and irrational laws, which, if they achieve the requisite efficacy, become valid laws. Although Spinoza states that "Civil laws, on the other hand, depend entirely on the decree of the commonwealth, and in order to maintain its freedom a commonwealth is bound to please nobody but itself, and to regard nothing as good or bad but what it decides to be good or bad for itself",[20] he notes that a state in which the laws are obeyed out of fear is not truly in a condition of peace but has merely achieved absence of war. For laws

---

[20] Wernham, *PT*, p. 305, Chap. 4, sect. 5. G. Vol. III, p. 294, 1. 6-9.

to be obeyed out of hope or respect for their promulgator, they must be just and rational laws; the sovereign himself has a duty to promulgate just laws in order to fulfill the end of the state, *viz.,* peace, harmony and security. "For it is certain, that seditions, wars, and contempt or breach of the laws are not so much to be imputed to the wickedness of the subjects, as to the bad state of a dominion."[21] Since the establishment of a secure civil order allows moral development of the sovereign as well as of the subjects, it is the sovereign's duty to enforce laws which the subjects can appreciate as advantageous, thereby strengthening the harmony of the state. "That the duty of him, who holds the dominion, is always to know its state and condition, to watch over the common welfare of all, and to execute whatever is to the interest of the majority of the subjects, is admitted by all."[22] When laws are in accordance with reason the state is that much more effective; at the far extremes of irrationality the ruler will lose his position as the head of the state insofar as power is allowed him by the citizens contingent on its proper use.

Since a well-organized state is more conducive to the moral development and ultimately the freedom of the citizens, the sovereign's obligation to promulgate just laws can be construed as a moral obligation. The achievement of the end of the state, *viz.,* harmony, within a context which allows the development of reason and freedom, requires an atmosphere of rationality which can be achieved only by the institution of rational laws. Since law is the primary instrument which the state uses to bring men to their fullest development, it is a moral duty on the part of the sovereign to enforce only those laws which are conducive to this end. As noted in the chapter on civil law, the sovereign is also obliged to restrain from introducing laws which tend towards excessive control of men's behavior insofar as these tend to bring the other laws into disrepute. Moral responsibility tied up with the sphere of civil law is not intrinsic to the law itself but comes into relevance with respect to the function of the sovereign as the leader of men in a state. The sovereign, as an individual or a group of individuals, is morally respons-

[21] Elwes, *PT*, p. 313, Chap. 5, sect. 2. G. Vol. III, p. 295.
[22] *Ibid.,* p. 328, Chap. 7, sect. 3. G. Vol. III, p. 308.

ible for promulgating just laws, although he may still retain sovereignty while promulgating bad laws if he does this within tolerable limits.

The sovereign is held to be exempt from the coercive force of the law, its sanction, since he is able to direct the power which enforces the law to relax its stipulations in his own case. If this is to be designated absolute sovereignty it must be recognized that it is of limited scope. Although the sovereign's power is absolute within certain limits, any attempt to transcend these boundaries will collapse the majesty of his power. These limits are assigned by the natural law of human nature which relates to the bounds beyond which legislation cannot be effective. Thus while the sovereign is exempt from the sanctions of civil law he is not exempt from the necessity of natural law which limits his power more narrowly than his will. "A sovereign is bound to observe the conditions of the contract for precisely the same reason as a man in the state of nature, in order that he may not be his own enemy, is bound to take care not to kill himself." [23] He is not able to promulgate and enforce whatever laws he wants although in what he is able to promulgate and enforce, his power, as derived from the concession of the subjects, is absolute. In short, the sovereign is above the coercive force of the civil law but it is not solely his will which determines that law. This conclusion must be modified to recognize the existence of fundamental civil laws, the foundations of the dominion (discussed in Chapter I, Sect. F) which, once established, cannot be revoked by the sovereign. "For the foundations of the dominion are to be considered as eternal decrees of the king, so that his ministers, entirely obey him in refusing to execute his orders, when he commands anything contrary to the same." [24]

E. THE RELATION BETWEEN LAW AND MORALITY

A legal system has a moral end. — Having established that it is possible for a law to be valid although unjust, the question arises again as to the end of law; whether law has in any sense a moral

[23] Wernham, *PT*, p. 307, Chap. 4, sect. 6. G. Vol. III, p. 294,.1. 26-29.
[24] Elwes, *PT*, p. 327, Chap. 7, sect. 1. G. Vol. III, p. 307.

end. This question refers to a legal system, not to the characteristics of particular laws. Since civil law is a tool which the state uses to bring about its end, that is, conditions of peace and harmony within which the individual citizens can pursue moral emendation, law functions as a means of the state. Law also has a definitive effect on the character of those subject to it: "The two last, i.e., laws and customs, are the only factors which can give a people a particular temperament, a particular nature, and lastly particular beliefs."[25]

With respect to its own end, law might be said to aim at rendering the enforcement of its threats unnecessary, that is, it aims at the obedience of those subject to it. Obedience may be rooted either in fear or in hope. Considering the end of the state, it becomes obvious that law aims at achieving obedience by inspiring the subject with positive feelings of hope, respect, reverence, etc. "For peace is not mere absence of war, but is a virtue that springs from force of character."[26] It is equally obvious that for this to be accomplished the laws must be such that people can approve, that is, they must offer to the subjects that which the subjects desire. In Spinoza's idiom, the law must promise each what is truly advantageous and what he can appreciate as advantageous although, for the most part, those subject to the law will not be fully rational. Spinoza never denies that this is the goal at which law should aim yet he recognizes that, since men are not fully rational, it is necessary to offer them another 'object', *viz.*, rewards and punishments, to induce them to understand that obedience is to their advantage. Law is a coercive system, but this is not to say that it can coerce men into doing anything at all. It is the job of the legislator and of law as an institution to determine the best way in which men can be led to do that which is truly advantageous although the subjects may not fully understand their true good.

Consideration of the precivil, though social, condition of men, the condition in which men are not subject to legal controls, may help clarify the notion of law as having a moral end. Men living without legal control, living simply according to the law of nature,

---

[25] Wernham, *TPT,* p. 181, Chap. 17. G. Vol. III, p. 217, 1. 21-24.
[26] Elwes, *PT,* p. 314, Chap. 5, sect. 4. G. Vol. III, p. 296.

are incapable of achieving fruitful and harmonious relations which have any permanence. This is analogous to Spinoza's conception of the international scene insofar as he denies the existence of authoritative legal control. In the comparatively unsettled precivil condition men do not have the opportunity, either in terms of motivation or of circumstance, to develop the spiritual and rational aspects of their nature. Nor can their natural powers be most productively used. The institution of the state, equipped with its most powerful tool, civil law, is taken to be the corrective of this situation. Men living within a state have available to them the circumstances and opportunities within which to develop their mental and physical natures. Thus they are able to more effectively fulfill their *conatus,* or their striving after perfection. Since this process of fulfillment is identical with moral development, civil law, as the primary tool of the state, is taken to serve a moral purpose or end. This is not to say that each particular law is directed toward a moral end but rather that law as an institution is so directed.

It must be recognized however that civil law is directed solely to the control of external behavior whereas morality is concerned with the motivation and understanding of the correctness of an act, that is, the internal aspect. Thus civil law cannot directly legislate morality but rather institutes those conditions of life which are conducive to the development of moral goodness in man, for example, congenial relations among the citizens, protection of certain areas of interest. There is not, and cannot be on principle, any direct legislation of morality. It ought to be noted that this is not a consequence of Spinoza's legal philosophy in particular but of any interpretation of law which recognizes, as it must, limitations to the scope of legal jurisdiction, and the sphere of morality as internal. Moral issues, however, may arise in the actual process of interpretation, application and enforcement of laws. Ascription of guilt and responsibility requires an interpretation of the facts of the case which rests implicitly on one's ethical view of man.[27]

---

[27] The seemingly amoral standard for application of the force of law based on what the prudent or reasonable man would do, in this writer's understanding, has packed into it certain moral standards for judging correct be-

Spinoza then is not subject to a standard criticism, typically applied to natural law theory, which appears to misfire with respect to the traditional natural law position as well — the contention that civil law attempts to legislate morality. It is held that if one claims to find a connection between law and morality, law will be placed in the position of legislating moral values and that this is not within the proper jurisdiction of law. Neither Spinoza nor the traditional natural law theorists fail to recognize the distinction between the internal and external spheres. Spinoza clearly recognizes that positive law cannot legislate morality yet requires that it institute conditions necessary for moral emendation. This point is adequately made in Spinoza's discussion of the ceremonial law of Moses, also a type of human or positive law. Spinoza distinguishes between the law of Moses which is geared to the temporal welfare of the state and that of Christ, geared to the spiritual blessedness of the individuals: "For Christ ... was not sent to preserve the state and establish laws, but to teach only the universal law. From this it is easily seen that Christ in no way abolished the law of Moses, for Christ had no wish to introduce any new laws into the state, his main object being to teach moral precepts and to distinguish them from the civil law."[28]

With reference to the question whether all laws should be directed towards a moral end, it is necessary to consider the issue of so-called neutral or amoral laws, laws which forbid or permit something which taken in itself is devoid of moral content or connotation.[29] Examples of laws which are morally indifferent would be traffic regulations — for example, rules determining which side of the road to drive on. It is clear that with respect to the security of the state, some regulations regarding traffic are necessary but there would seem not to be any moral issue involved in the choice of the

---

havior. If this is not admitted, it is contended that the standard would not be amoral but immoral. This point is developed in Chap. V, Sect. C.
[28] Wernham, *TPT,* p. 91, Chap. 5. G. Vol. III, pp. 70-71, 1. 33-35.
[29] This situation is parallel to Spinoza's notion of the ceremonial law which denotes behavior, originally indifferent, as right or wrong, e.g. the taboo in the Jewish code against eating pork, marriage at certain times of the year, etc.

details. Yet these laws function as other civil laws, that is, by the enforcement of the sanctions consequent on disobedience. This consideration is not a serious problem for Spinoza's theory insofar as he does not claim that every law must be a just or moral law.

Although the details of the neutral laws cannot be judged as moral or immoral, the existence or non-existence of such laws is an ethical question, *viz.*, it is conducive to the harmony and security of the state to have laws which, for example, regulate traffic. Again the distinction must be kept in mind between a body of laws or a legal system, and particular laws within that system since it is quite possible and defensible to claim certain properties for a system as a whole which are not shared by each particular member of that system. It is contended that the moral or ethical purpose of law is referable to a legal system as a whole but not necessarily to each particular law. Law as a civil institution has a definite aim although particular laws might not serve any function except to fill in the gap where some law is needed. Once the laws are established as laws however, each has a duty to obey them as strict as the duty to obey any other law.

Spinoza recognizes that there are certain morally desirable conditions which are not within reach of civil legislation. As noted above, law deals with actions, that is, external aspects of behavior, whereas the proper sphere of morality is internal. There are many situations and conditions which law does not approve, e.g., dishonesty, but it is not within its power to do anything about it unless there is an external manifestation of the condition which affects other people. "Besides, men of leisure never lack the wit to get round laws which are framed to deal with things which cannot be forbidden absolutely, things like feasting, gambling, personal adornment, and so forth, which are bad only in excess, and must be judged as excessive or otherwise in relation to the wealth of each individual, so that no general law can determine what is excessive and what is not."[30] Law also in its application deals with cases in which both parties are morally blameless; it is necessary however to make a decision in favor of one of them. The act which is punish-

---

[30] Wernham, *PT*, p. 435, Chap. 10, sect. 5. G. Vol. III, p. 355, 1. 29-33.

ed is morally neutral yet any legal code requires that a decision be made.[31]

A legal system may be unjust. — The issue must finally be raised of the possibility that a system of laws may be fundamentally unjust. Until this point in the analysis of Spinoza's position it has been assumed that it is impossible to have a valid, i.e., sufficiently efficacious, system of laws which did not meet definite ethical requirements. This assumption, although central to the development of Spinoza's legal theory, seems to be neither substantiated by nor consistent with certain other of his general principles. Although there is an important distinction between that which is truly to men's advantage and that which men think is to their advantage, it is possible to conceive of a system of laws which men accept as advantageous but which in fact is not. Such a system might achieve the requisite obedience, and since laws are not invalidated because they are evil, there could be a valid system which is manifestly unjust. It is necessary to consider further whether, within the framework of Spinoza's philosophy, it is allowable to contend that an unjust system might appeal to the majority as a good or advantageous system. It is certainly true that an unjust law, a particular iniquitous rule, can and often does appeal to a man as advantageous. Spinoza himself recognizes this in the *Ethics* in his plea to men to transcend the level of the lower satisfactions and attain an understanding of their true advantage.

However unjust a valid legal system is taken to be it can never enforce certain commands, for example, conditions instituting the cessation of liberty of thought. This limitation to the possible scope of efficacious legislation refers to Spinoza's recognition of basic natural powers of human nature. Men are incapable of conceiving that legislation which attempted to annul the free expression of these powers could possibly be to their advantage. However a large

---

[31] Spinoza does not discuss laws which do not function coercively as commands but rather state procedures for performing certain legal acts, e.g., marriage contracts, wills. One does not 'break' these laws in the sense of incurring penalties; rather if the procedure is not followed correctly the contract or will is invalid.

spectrum of evil possibilities remains which a legal system could theoretically enforce and it must be shown, on Spinoza's principles, that there is some impossibility in this notion if it is to be maintained that a legal system of necessity serves a moral function in the state. The system, it is granted, will never achieve total or complete injustice insofar as there remain certain rights or powers which a man cannot cede; however within these limits a legal system can embody substantial injustice.

A possible way to avoid or at least modify this conclusion may be considered: if a legal system of a state is viewed, not in terms of its own isolated integrity but as a tool of the state, it can be asked whether the state can achieve its end if its system of laws is unjust. The function of the state being to produce conditions which are conducive to the moral emendation and freedom of the individual, the state is said to do wrong when it does that which is against its nature, that which causes its own destruction, i.e., that which does not coincide with the natural laws relating to men in society. Thus a state could not achieve its end if its legal system is unjust, i.e., not directed to the advantage of the subjects. "It is impossible for a multitude to be guided, as it were, by one mind, as under dominion is required, unless it has laws ordained according to the dictate of reason."[32] "This unity of mind can in no wise be conceived, unless the commonwealth pursues chiefly the very end, which sound reason teaches is to the interest of all men."[33] It is not feasible then to defend an unjust code of laws as a means to the achievement of the end of the state, which is ultimately a moral end, since it has turned out, on Spinoza's principles, that a state could not achieve its end under these conditions.

Spinoza holds that the state is strong in proportion to the rationality of its dictums, and weak in proportion to their irrationality. Although weak, the state may nevertheless exist which aims, within certain limits, at an evil end. The irrational state, being weaker, is less stable, yet as noted above the subjects do have an absolute duty of obedience to its laws.

---

[32] Elwes, *PT,* p. 298, Chap. 2, sect. 21. G. Vol. III, p. 283.
[33] *Ibid.,* p. 303-304, Chap. 3, sect. 7. G. Vol. III, p. 287.

There is no intrinsic connection between law and morality. — If the above is accepted as the final turn of the argument, Spinoza has not made out a case for an intrinsic connection between law and morality. The indicated points of contact between law and morality must be taken as recommended rather than as necessary. Each point of contact between law and morality noted above must be modified in the direction away from conclusiveness. That is, a particular unjust law cannot be justified on the basis of the fact that it is part of a legal system. The legal system might itself be unjust and it cannot be justified on the grounds that it is a means to the achievement of the moral ends of the state. An unjust system will not allow the state to achieve its end.

Spinoza contends that the existence of the civil state always has a moral value since the state brings men out of the pre-civil, barbaric condition in which there is no possibility of moral emendation. A state with an unjust legal code has a very limited value indeed, none of which is drawn from its legal structure; yet it has a certain value, insofar as it has a definite control over the relations of men with each other through extra-legal means of organization and persuasion, e.g., social codes and customs. Spinoza clearly recognizes that there is an essential difference between a good state and a bad state. The only point being made here is that any state is better than no state. The claim that any laws are better than no laws cannot however be substantiated with equal justice, although Spinoza himself would seem to be making this point. An unjust system of laws is a definite hindrance to a state which may however be compensated to some extent through the efficacy of other social institutions.

There is in civil law a minimal necessary content. — Although the content of law is not determined by ethical standards, Spinoza does recognize the necessity of a certain minimal content in a functioning legal system. "Since it is the function of the sovereign alone to decide what is necessary for the welfare of the whole people and the security of the state, and to command accordingly, it is also the function of the sovereign alone to decide how everyone should practise piety towards his neighbor, i.e., how everyone should obey

God."[34] Thus law must deal with those things connected with the public welfare, the safety of the state, the duty of men towards neighbors, and the manner of obeying God.

It cannot however be maintained that the manner in which the law deals with these points is of necessity just or right. This depends on the level of reason of the multitude which determines what they will allow the sovereign to enforce as law directed to their advantage. In a totalitarian dictator-state, for example, the public welfare might be interpreted to entail protecting the citizens by ridding the state of an undesired minority. This, according to Spinoza's notion of justice as rendering to each man his own, would be a manifestly unjust program, albeit legally organized and enforced. If it is attempted to demonstrate that men could not conceive of such injustices as being to their advantage to the point where they obey the laws, it is perhaps sufficient to recall the political history of the twentieth century alone as adequate to count against such a claim. It is a different point to recognize that men might not obey such laws if it were not for the sanctions attached. Law is that instrument of social control which works through sanctions and therefore to note that the law might not 'work' if it were not for the sanction attached is tantamount in this instance to saying that the law might not work if it were not a law.

Spinoza's recognition that a legal system must deal with certain aspects of social relationships and of an individual's relation with God is a purely formal requirement of a necessary content in a legal system. There are certain aspects of human behavior which can and must come under the jurisdiction of law if a legal system is to function as a legal system, that is, as a system which controls those areas of human behavior relevant to the preservation of the state. However the system can as well function to preserve a bad state as a good one. Although there is a broad stipulation of a required content in a legal system, this does not guarantee that particular laws will handle this control in a just manner. It might turn out, on further analysis of human nature, that there is a certain overlap of necessary laws with just laws, in the way that there is a definite

[34] Wernham, *TPT*, p. 213, Chap. 19. G. Vol. III, p. 232, 1. 23-28.

overlap of impossible laws with unjust laws. For example, it might be the case that legislation with a view to the security of the state requires laws which protect or aim at protecting the citizens from external enemies. This, as a law which protects certain rights, can be said to aim at justice. The manner of achieving this protection however might be unjust, as for example, draft laws for military service based on principles of partiality.

In short, a legal system must incorporate a minimal content comprising whatever is necessary for the existence and preservation of men in a state. If this condition is not fulfilled the legal structure and thus the form of the state would collapse. There are certain conditions that a legal system must establish if it is to function as regulative of behavior, for example, a legal system must preserve what has been called formal justice, the application of laws to individuals insofar as they are relevant. This requirement is merely formal however in that it ultimately rests with the sovereign or his delegated court to determine which circumstances are considered extenuating.

There is a necessary connection between civil law and natural law. — Spinoza's conception of the necessary relation between civil law and natural law does not entail a guarantee of the material justice of a legal system. It is simply the recognition that law, as an instrument geared to function in the natural world, must fulfill certain requirements embodied in the natural law of human beings. This requirement is comprised by the necessity not to promulgate laws which deny the free expression of certain basic powers of man, e.g., freedom of thought or belief.

Outside of these predetermined limits, however, it is possible for unjust laws to be promulgated and obeyed in a state which is not completely rational, although in a state which is completely rational, there could not be injustice of any kind. Spinoza's philosophy of the state however is not utopian — he does not deny that a state which is less than perfect could exist as a state. Insofar as this is admitted, it must also be admitted that unjust laws could achieve the required efficacy through the obedience of citizens who have a mistaken notion of their own advantage, or who obey from fear of the sanctions which a less than totally rational sovereign has the power and the will to enforce. Spinoza also recognizes as a natural necessity that a legal system include all laws requisite for the preservation of the state, but this need not necessarily be rational or just legislation. Thus in Spinoza's opinion certain unjust commands may be laws but not all unjust commands may be laws. The reason that not all unjust commands of the sovereign can be laws is not that there is an intrinsic connection between law and morality but rather a natural limitation to those things a man can be coerced into doing.

Spinoza's recognition of a definite though minimal limit to the content of possible legislation indicates an important characteristic of human institutions which are after all subject to the condition of harmonizing with certain given laws of human nature. If such natural laws are denied, the denial could be no more than a verbal point; to disallow laws of human conduct and behavior is to render man impotent. To study legal institutions within the frame of a larger whole, *viz.*, the natural world, helps focus both the instrumentality of the system and its natural limitations. This approach hinges on the recognition of a necessary but amoral natural law or, in the contemporary idiom, generic traits of human nature. This allows the recognition that there are certain natural limits to theoretically possible legal systems without being forced to claim material justice for the systems.

There is an important level of reasonableness in Spinoza's position, although, if the above is a fair analysis, he himself did not recognize the full consequences of his own principles. Although the tone and intention of his writings tend toward a more definitive relation between law and morality than is actually substantiated by his analysis, this is not necessarily a mistake. He did not present a separate thesis on the nature of law, which, it would seem, would have suffered from inconsistencies, but rather incorporated his remarks within political treatises which, in spite of his care, do have a polemical dimension. This also is not necessarily a mistake — it is ultimately a question of how one receives the remarks. That Spinoza was anxious to present the structure of a rational or just state is clear enough; that he has not in fact argued satisfactorily for this intrinsic connection between law and morality is perhaps to be attributed to his occasional tendency to consider human endeavors as if men were fully rational, though he knows in truth that they are not.

V

PROBLEMS OF LEGAL THEORY

Although Spinoza's legal philosophy, perhaps because of its fragmentary and non-systematic character, has had little direct influence on legal theorists, it is believed that his approach and certain of his basic ideas can be put to good use in dealing with problems of legal philosophy. This chapter suggests a scheme for analyzing the significance of several of Spinoza's insights with respect to six problems of legal philosophy.

A. THE PROBLEM OF THE EVALUATION OF LAW

It is certainly obvious to legal theorists that judgments of the goodness and badness of civil laws are constantly being made; thus the question inevitably arises as to the validity or cognitive value of such judgments. The concern is primarily with the criteria assumed in the evaluation rather than with the correctness or incorrectness of a particular judgment. If the standard is merely subjective the cognitive value of a particular judgment is admittedly nominal.[1]

---

[1] Cf. Hans Kelsen, *General Theory of Law and State,* Chap. I, where he notes that the pure theory of law cannot decide whether a law is just. Judgments of value are taken to be subjective and relative, determined by emotional factors and have no place in a scientific theory. In "The Pure Theory of Law" he states, "The Pure Theory of Law separates the concept of the legal completely from that of the moral norm and establishes the law as a specific system independent even of the moral law." Subjective relativism is also exemplified by Radbruch (*Rechtsphilosophie*) and Jellinek (*Die Sozialethische Bedeutung von Recht, Unrecht und Strafe*).

Even if it is accepted that standards defined within an objective ethical system are available, these notions of goodness and badness have not always been considered relevant to civil law.[2] A distinction must be made here between the essence or nature of law and judgments imposed upon the law. It may be true that ethical characteristics are not intrinsic to law itself; yet it is certainly legitimate and necessary to judge human institutions (such as legal systems) in ethical terms. It is indeed possible to seek objective standards which are relevant for evaluating law without maintaining that the goodness of a law is a criterion of its validity, that is, characteristic of the essence of law.[3]

On the other hand, there is no necessary connection between objective standards of evaluation and the notion of deriving positive law from *a priori* laws of reason or a natural law.

Spinoza's legal philosophy allows for the distinction between the validity (existence) of a law and the goodness of a law. He offers a theory of the essence of law which, as previously claimed, allows objective judgment of the value of laws. That is, law is conceived in such a way that it is possible to apply standards of criticism to particular commands whose value is in question. Goodness and badness are defined with respect to the nature of man; they are notions relative to human nature and its powers. However these notions achieve an objective status insofar as it is maintained that the characterization of man's essence is universally applicable to all members of the class. The notion of 'good for man' can then be applied to civil laws in order to determine the ethical value of a

---

[2] Cf. John Austin, in *Lectures on Jurisprudence* (Vol. II) where he distinguishes between the science of (positive) law and the science of legislation (objective judgment of laws): "As principles abstracted from positive systems are the subject of general jurisprudence, so is the exposition of such principles its exclusive or appropriate object. With the goodness or badness of laws, as tried by the test of utility . . . it has no immediate concern" (p. 1107).
[3] The need for objective evaluation of law has been recognized in recent literature by such writers as Morris R. Cohen (*Reason and Nature*, Bk. 3, Ch. 4), Benjamin Cardozo (*Paradoxes of Legal Science*, Ch. 2), Roscoe Pound (*Law and Morals*), Prof. Ernest Nagel ("On the Fusion of Fact and Value: A Reply to Professor Fuller"), German Interessenjurisprudenz (*The Jurisprudence of Interests*, cf. esp. articles by Isay and Heck).

given law, that is, whether it fulfills the purpose of law with respect to the development of human nature and its powers.

To make legitimate judgments of the goodness or badness of laws does not require holding the view that the universe is intrinsically teleologic. However it is believed that law, regarded as a means to the achievement of a certain end, must be taken to have a particular function or purpose, if standards of evaluation are to be applicable. If law is denied a purpose, if it is characterized in merely formal terms (e.g., as a body of rules derived from a basic norm),[4] it is not possible to distinguish good rules from bad ones. And if there is no basis for an evaluation, there can be no legitimate evaluation.

Spinoza consistently recognizes that law is a social institution with a definite aim and purpose with respect to the goals of man and society. Within this framework it is possible to determine objective standards for judging laws by relating the notion of the purpose of law as social institution to general ethical standards. A law need not fulfill this purpose however in order to be a valid law, that is, valid laws are not necessarily good laws.

It is believed that in order to allow objective evaluation of law it is necessary to hold that law has a discernible purpose or end. The function of law in its normative dimension, however, need not be identified with the essence of law, either as totally or partially definitive. Thus a particular law which does not fulfill the ethical purpose of law is not *ipso facto* invalidated. The rationale for holding purpose as characteristic of law is based on the belief that denial of this requirement reduces legal theory to purely formal analysis, which, in its speculative freedom lacks any characteristic or determinable relation to actual legal systems. Such formal theories are substantially useless as guides to the development or improvement of actual legal systems.

This issue can be re-phrased in terms of the distinction between natural (moral) justice and legal justice.[5] Is there a standard of absolute (moral) justice independent of and prior to standards

---

[4] Cf. Kelsen, "The Pure Theory of Law".
[5] For an introductory discussion of this problem see Aristotle, *Nichomachean Ethics*, Bk. V.

defined by particular (legal) systems? or are values simply the expression of a subjective will or ideologies grounded solely in non-cognitive will-projection? This way of putting the question initiates a forced dilemma by seeming to allow no choice between the two horns: either one takes an absolutist stand which is questionable from the fact of its ultimate dependence on *a priori* rules and a teleological metaphysics; or one is forced into subjectivism or non-cognitivism which is useless with respect to forming judgments that carry any compelling character. A third approach,[6] which will be designated objective relativism, allows the recognition of standards of justice independent of *a priori* rules, teleological claims or voluntaristic ethics. Spinoza's ethical and legal philosophy exemplifies this path, as does naturalistic ethics for the most part.

Implicit in Spinoza's analysis is a distinction between legal justice and what will be called moral justice. (The expression 'natural' justice is avoided here — in favor of 'moral' justice — the former being regarded as having unfortunate association with natural law.) Legal justice, rendering to each man his own, in its application to particular cases is an ethically empty formula requiring positive law itself to delimit by statute or precedent the content of the notion of 'one's own'. There is no guarantee that the area designated will coincide with anyone's sense of moral justice. Moral justice, in Spinoza's philosophy, refers to the definition of good with respect to the moral emendation of man, the development of his specific powers (virtues). Thus ethical standards are applicable in evaluating a legal system conceived as an instrument devised by men to institute the conditions necessary for the achievement of rationality and freedom. Legal justice need not necessarily coincide with moral justice in any given legal system; that is, it is possible for a law to be both valid and (morally) unjust.

It is in the final analysis not possible for a philosophy of law to guarantee that all laws will be just laws except (1) if the theory introduces the dogmatic and confusing identification of law with

---

[6] Professor Nagel's debate with Prof. Fuller presents a thorough discussion of this issue, Natural Law Forum, 1958.

'good' law, that is, the identification of legality with moral justice;[7] or (2) if a theory ignores standards of justice which are independent of actual positive law, that is, the reduction of moral justice to legal justice.[8] The first position is characteristic of absolutist theories (exclusive focus on reason); the second of voluntarist theories (exclusive focus on will).

The intermediary position which Spinoza adopts hinges on a theory of human nature which recognizes the interplay of reason and will. The notion of a rational will — will mediated by reason — introduces the key question, Desire for what? At this point it is possible to evaluate a command of law by asking, Command for what? This question refers again to the purpose of law as to whether it is fulfilling its function with respect to the desires of the rational will. This is not a particularly easy question to answer, and the evidence needed is of an extremely complex nature; what is important however is that evidence is available in any particular case and one can know what kind of information is relevant. This makes it possible to substantiate an evaluation of the goodness or badness of a particular law.

B. THE PROBLEM OF THE SOURCE OF LAW

The notion of the will as the source of law is generally associated with the command theory of law;[9] while the notion of reason as the source of law is traditionally tied up with natural law theory.[10] The consequences of these points will be briefly analyzed.

[7] Cf. Aquinas, *Summa Theologica,* Part I of the Second Part, Ques. 95: "As Augustine says (De. Lib. Arb. i, 5), "that which is not just seems to be no law at all"; therefore the force of a law depends on the extent of its justice ... But if in any point it (human law) differs from the law of nature, it is no longer a law but a corruption of law."

[8] The earliest expression of this view in the Western heritage occurs in the Sophists' identification of justice with the will of the stronger. Cf. Plato's *Republic,* Bk. I.

[9] This position is exemplified by Hobbes (*Leviathan,* Part II, Ch. 26) and by the Austinian school of jurisprudence. Conversely it has been recognized, e.g., by Korkunov in his *General Theory of Law* (Bk. I, Ch. II), that rules of law are commands but do not emanate from an individual will.

[10] Among proponents of this view are the Stoics, Cicero, the Scholastics, Grotius and Kant. Cf. Appendix A for a discussion of natural law.

To hold that law is a product of reason is to claim that there is a rational basis to every law. The claim goes further in intimating that the reason or the rational basis is a good reason, that it exhibits a rational or intelligent apprehension of the purpose of the law and of law in general. This need not necessarily include the notion that the purpose or end of law is implicit in the universe. The teleological claim is an attempt at metaphysical justification of the belief that a rational law fulfills a moral end but this can as well be substantiated in terms of any individual writer's conception of law. If law is taken to have an intrinsic purpose, it follows that this purpose must be known somehow to the promulgator since law, as a product of reason, could not be decreed in the absence of this knowledge. The double sense of reason here, as both a faculty of mind, and as rational and intelligent (reasoned) awareness suggests the claim that law, as a product of reason, must be rational. And to be rational or correct is to coincide with the essential aim of law. Since reason is the faculty which leads the mind to truth, law which is a product of reason, is specifically identified with true or correct law.

On the other hand, if law is taken to be the product of will, no initial stricture of rationality is imposed on it. It is theoretically conceivable that a sovereign may will anything at all and promulgate this as a law. The definition of law as a command is derivable from this; law is taken to be the sanctioned will of the sovereign to the effect that someone or some group do, or refrain from doing, something. It is assumed that the sovereign has the power to enforce his will, however arbitrary it may be, that is, the sovereign holds the superior power in the community. The conjunction of the notion of law as a product of the will with the notion of law as a command stands in contrast to the conjunction of the notion of law as a product of reason with the notion of law as fulfilling a moral or rational purpose.

Spinoza also conceives of law as produced by the will of the sovereign. There are indications however, e.g., the definition of law as a 'plan of living', that this view does not require defining law as a command of the will. To decipher this point it is necessary to consider Spinoza's view of the nature of reason and the will, or in his idiom, of the intellect and the will. According to Spinoza the will and the intellect are the same thing, "the individual volitions and ideas themselves".[11] "By the 'will' I understand a faculty of affirming or denying, but not a desire — a faculty, I say, by which the mind affirms or denies that which is true or false, and not a desire by which the mind seeks a thing or turns away from it."[12] It is to be noted that "these faculties are universal notions which are not distinguishable from the individual notions from which they are formed".[13] For Spinoza the will as a universal idea does not exist. Volitions are particular ideas which are affirmed or denied and there is no distinction between the power of understanding and the power of willing.

Thus since law is held to be a product of will this is tantamount to having it as a product of thinking and judging. This introduces the element of rationality, or at least eliminates the arbitrariness of an 'absolute faculty of willing or not willing'. "In the mind there is no volition or affirmation and negation except that which the idea, in so far as it is an idea, involves."[14] Thus the will of the sovereign, that is, laws, are not consecrations of the sovereign's desires but rather the ideas which he affirms. The goodness or badness of the laws will depend on whether these affirmed ideas are adequate or inadequate, true or false. However from the fact that the will is in some sense identical with the intellect it does not follow that all laws are necessarily rational. The will may very well be misguided since reason is not taken to be equivalent to true reason.

It is possible then in Spinoza's view to conceive of law as issuing from the will of the sovereign and yet having certain limits insofar as the will is not a distinct faculty; it is not free and unmediated desire, but is governed by natural causality. If law is taken to be a command it is nonetheless rooted in a thinking process and thus it is possible to distinguish with respect to the notion of law itself, good and bad law. Law, as the affirmed and enforced ideas or thoughts of the sovereign, can be evaluated according to the general criteria for ideas, that is, epistemological criteria. To judge the

[11] *E, op. cit.*, Part II, Prop. 49, Dem. G. Vol. II, p. 131.
[12] *Ibid.*, Part II, Prop. 48, Note. G. Vol. II, pp. 129-130.
[13] *Ibid.*, G. Vol. II, p. 130.
[14] *E, op. cit.*, Part II, Prop. 49. G. Vol. II, p. 130.

rightness of a law it is not necessary to introduce external criteria; rather judgment requires determining whether the volition or idea is adequate or inadequate. A law is not necessarily good by reason of its source, but there is an objective criterion stemming from the source to determine if it is good or bad. Thus it is not so much the command aspect (will) nor true reason that is the essence of law as it is a program or 'plan' developed by the sovereign mind which governs through sanctioned command the behavior of others. The plan need not be fully rational, although for reasons noted above, it cannot be totally irrational.

Perhaps it would be fair to say that for Spinoza it is necessary that laws cannot be totally irrational but that these laws are not necessarily, although they ought to be, products of a rational will. This is the recognition, from another point of view, that the sovereign ought to be rational, although he need not be, provided he does not attempt in his legislation to go beyond the possibilities designated by the natural law. Since the rational man is, for Spinoza, identical with the good man, it follows that, ideally, legislation should issue from a just and rational will, but this is not a necessary condition for a law to achieve validity. However the law itself must attain a certain minimum of reasonableness in order to exact obedience, notwithstanding the fact that it might very well have been promulgated for the wrong, i.e., unjust, reasons. If one would want to argue here that a reasonable law can be the product of a rational will only, this would seem to confound the source with the result, and thus fall into the genetic fallacy in order to make the point.

C. THE PROBLEM OF JUDICIAL LEGISLATION

Contemporary jurisprudence recognizes the need of objective standards for evaluating laws not only, as it were, after the fact, but also as guides in the legislative process itself. The problem is generally discussed with respect to the judicial process insofar as it is generally agreed that judges do not, in fact, cannot mechanically apply pre-existing rules or mechanically determine all cases by appeal to precedent.[15] The recognition of the element of interpretation involved in applying the law introduces the question of the basis of the interpretation.

Without considering whether judges should legislate[16] or whether all law is judge-made law,[17] it will be acknowledged in this discussion that they in fact do make law. Recent writing concerning the judicial process tends to concur in the contention that the necessity of judicial legislation is not due to inadequacies in actual legal systems.[18] Laws must be formulated in general and often ambiguous terms which cannot on principle be particularized if the law is to have directive force. The element of necessary interpretation in the application of law forces the judge into a legislative capacity. To improvise on Wittgenstein's example: What is or is not a cow is for the judge to decide.

If this analysis is accepted it is obvious that a judge requires some standards to aid him in making decisions. No one has yet declared that law is the arbitrary will of the judges, except by way of criticism, which interestingly enough would be taken as a real defect of a legal system. The question arises then as to how the law ought to be interpreted, the standards on which to base legislation. This question refers to all stages of the legislative process but will be handled in this discussion with respect to the task of the judges. The only reason for this focus is an interest in dealing with legal problems as they are outlined in contemporary literature, although it is recognized that Spinoza was not dealing with the common law tradition in his legal theory.

---

[15] Cf. Cardozo, *The Nature of the Judicial Process;* M. R. Cohen, *Law and the Social Order,* pp. 112-148; Holmes, "Path of the Law"; Pound, "The Ideal Element in American Judicial Decision" for a discussion of this issue.

[16] Cf. Bentham for an attack on judicial legislation. Also see Stone, pp. 149 ff. for a discussion of the interesting case of the French Code which in 1790 forbid the judges to interpret the law.

[17] Cf. Gray, *The Nature and Sources of Law,* Ch. IV, for a discussion of the notion that all law is judge-made law. Also Holmes, "The Path of the Law".

[18] Cf. H. L. A. Hart, "Positivism and the Separation of Law and Morals" for a discussion of the error of formalism and the necessity of judicial interpretation. For a lack of recognition of this point see Montesquieu, *The Spirit of the Laws,* Vol. I, Bk. 6, Ch. 3, 4.

Three types of theories have been offered: the claim that the judge must refer to the will of the legislator[19] and the claim that the judge must appeal to *a priori* standards of material justice or natural laws[20] both suffer from similar defects. The simplest criticism of both the voluntarist and the natural law positions is that neither the will of the legislator nor the relevant natural law are necessarily discoverable; in fact, they may not exist as such. A third type of theory[21] introduces the notion of the reasonable man, the prudent man, the average man, public opinion, social interests, etc., as standards on which to base decisions. It is contended that such criteria require in the final analysis reference to ethical standards, minimally the notion that what the rational, prudent or average man, or public opinion endorses is right or just. An amoral standard for judging the rightness or wrongness of human conduct is impossible. Thus it is necessary to determine objective ethical standards, the only feasible alternative being the arbitrary introduction of subjective standards by each judge or group of judges.

A theory such as Spinoza's which recognizes objective standards on which to base value judgments of actual legal systems offers a legitimate basis for legislation and judicial decisions as well as relevant grounds for criticism. Spinoza himself recognizes that application of law involves interpretation, i.e., legislation, and thus notes that if legislation is to be traceable to the sovereign, this function must be entrusted to a group designated by him as his representative.

Since Spinoza allows for the possibility of law being both valid and evil, it is of interest to note that judge-made law could conceivably function to alleviate some of the evils of the existing law by selective application and 'judicial' interpretation. This offers significant enrichment of the notion of law as a self-corrective sys-

---

[19] This position is endorsed by those theorists who claim that all law is the will of the sovereign, e.g., Austin, *Province of Jurisprudence Determined,* Lecture I, p. 104.
[20] For a recent discussion of this position cf. Fuller, "Positivism and Fidelity to Law — a Reply to Professor Hart."
[21] Cf. Cardozo, *Paradoxes of Legal Science,* ch. 3; Ehrlich, *Fundamental Principles of the Sociology of Law,* ch. 15; and Pound's writings, for a discussion of this approach.

tem, without depending on such quasi-metaphysical notions as inevitable progress in social life,[22] or the notion of the state which in time approaches the embodiment of the absolute.[23] If judicial legislation can be referred to a set of objective ethical standards, legal theorists need not be constrained to relegate the judge to a supposedly non-legislative role. The usual fear is that an allowed deviation from the status quo can only sanction the arbitrary and questionable will of a group of men who after all do have their own interests. These final points tie up with a further problem in legal theory developed directly below.

D. THE PROBLEM OF STABILITY AND CHANGE IN THE LAW

It is important to distinguish two types of social change: the change within actual social circumstances and the change characteristic of social consciousness with respect to ideals and interests. The two levels do not necessarily develop simultaneously. If this distinction is not noted criticism runs the risk of indulging in critiques of theories which have never been held. For example, theorists are fond of criticizing natural law doctrine for the naive belief that absolute standards of justice and evaluation are applicable irrespective of time or place, whereas it is perfectly obvious that situations and circumstances are constantly in flux.[24]

It is perfectly obvious and no theory, no matter how utopian, has ever denied the fact of social change. Nor need an absolutist deny such truths in order to make his point — *viz.,* that there are universal immutable standards of justice — although, as noted above, absolutism suffers from other real and significant defects. On the other hand, utilitarians and pragmatists (American Legal Realists) have often been criticized on equally misguided grounds: it is contended that they ignore the pattern and continuity exhibited

---

[22] Important proponents of this view are Spencer, Compte and Durkheim.
[23] This is a typically Hegelian theory, although Hegel himself did not deny the value of the individual.
[24] Cf. Kelsen, "Natural Law Doctrine and Legal Positivism" in *General Theory of Law and State* regarding his view of the static nature of natural law as a conservative ideology introduced to justify and absolutize positive law.

in the perennial ideals of justice and equity in order to stress the need for change and progress.[25] This certainly is not true — the utilitarian and the pragmatist are interested rather in adjusting ethical notions to correspond with changed social circumstances and social interests. However confused the criticism, there is significant disagreement between those who contend that there are absolute ethical norms which are universally applicable to any particular situation, and those who believe that moral standards are historically and sociologically conditioned or, at the extreme, relative to each individual. This question is important for legal theory insofar as its answer will substantiate the case for or against the value of change in the law. That change in actual laws is always necessary to deal with changed circumstances is unquestionable; however the degree of latitude or flexibility allowed or recommended will be determined by one's notion of the absoluteness or historicity of standards of justice.

Spinoza it is believed offers a good beginning here. He recognizes the need for definite stability or a stable core in the law in his discussion of the function of fundamental laws as the foundation of the dominion. All legislation of the state must be in harmony with these basic laws which define the form or legal structure of the state. However since laws must structure the state in a manner which satisfies the citizens, at least to the extent necessary to assure the obedience needed to validate them as laws, as the level of understanding or rationality of a people fluctuates different laws will appeal to them as advantageous. Thus there will be a corresponding fluctuation in the content of the commands which can be enforced. In broad socio-political terms this assures that legislation will be roughly geared to the notion of justice prevalent in a majority. Spinoza appreciates democracy for precisely this point: legislation in a democracy tends to remain closer to the will of the people, and the unchangeable fundamental laws tend to be interpreted by reference to changing social consciousness.

---

[25] Cf. E. T. Mitchell, "Social Ideals and the Law". For a discussion of the problems and merits of natural right theory and of pragmatism with respect to the question of stability and change in the law, see W. B. Kennedy, "Pragmatism as a Philosophy of Law".

However Spinoza's recognition of certain constant characteristics of human nature guarantees a minimal though important set of necessary principles which any legal system must incorporate. These conditions are comprised by the natural law of human beings which is both necessary and universal. Thus there are circumscribed limits defining the class of commands which can become valid laws — limits which are not essentially dependent on actual circumstances or historic conditions but which are intrinsically related to human nature.

There is then a necessary and permanent core in all legal systems as well as natural limits which define the boundaries of possible legislation. However this stipulation of a necessary content and of a general class of void 'laws' has no intrinsic relation to notions of unchanging ethical ideals, manifested throughout history, as a necessary condition of legality. Since for Spinoza the natural law is essentially amoral, it is perfectly possible for legal systems bound by natural conditions to include unjust laws — in other words, a valid law may be unjust. Yet Spinoza recognizes that it is not possible for a legal system to incorporate laws which are not considered 'just' by the majority of citizens. This recognition hinges on the requirement of efficacy coupled with the incapacity of human beings to act against their conception of their own advantage.

Thus Spinoza's analysis of law and human nature would guarantee the ethical goodness of all laws only if one held a subjectivist ethics. On the principles of Spinoza's ethics however there is no necessary relation between valid and just laws, except in the extreme and hypothetical case of a totally rational population whose understanding of justice would coincide with true justice.

Thus with respect to the problem of stability and change, Spinoza recognizes both the necessity of a definite minimal content in all legal systems — the recognition of stability — and the existence of a large area of laws relative to historically conditioned notions of justice and historically unique circumstances, yet limited ultimately by the boundaries of human flexibility — the recognition of change. There is no necessary ethical content although there is the formal requirement that laws appear just to the citizens.

Spinoza's analysis allows the discussion of stability and change implicit in legal development to be referred to the wider question of the conditions requisite for change in law, *viz.*, change in historical circumstances and change in ethical consciousness. Change or stability per se are neither good nor bad, that is, change cannot be *a priori* identified with progress, nor stability with security. The question of the value of change and stability refers to the conception of advantage that is behind the desire for change or stability. Ultimately this ties up with an analysis of the level of ethical consciousness achieved by the multitude.

Implicit in Spinoza's analysis is the recommendation that men strive to achieve higher levels of rationality. This development carries with it a gradual change in the content of law with respect to the changing conception of justice — perhaps asymptotically, although not necessarily, approaching true justice.

E. THE PROBLEM OF THE LIMITS TO SOVEREIGNTY AND THE JURISDICTION OF LAW

Recent political history as well as a general consciousness of the integrity and value of the individual has helped to renew interest in the question of the limits to sovereign power and the sphere of jurisdiction of law. This issue can be divided at the outset into two distinct questions: the one question of the proper (just) limits to sovereign power and the proper (just) sphere of legal jurisdiction; and the different question of the LEGAL (positive) limits to sovereign power and the LEGAL (positive) sphere of the jurisdiction of law. Although analytically distinguishable it may be contended that these two ways of putting the question ultimately coincide. Once this distinction is made, however, the question arises of what sense can be made of the notion of legal limitations imposed on a legislator and on a legal system, along with the different question of the validity of an unjust law and the rights of an unjust sovereign.

At first glance it appears absurd to speak of legal limitations as applicable to a legislator or a legal system and such a notion has often been dismissed as incredible.[26] The consequences of this dismissal are particularly significant if, in addition, extra-legal limitations are also denied; one is thereby constrained to posit the notion of an absolute sovereign who has unlimited authority. It can be argued however that in actual fact there are perfectly good examples of legal systems so limited: for example, the Constitution of the United States (a legal document) imposes a limit on the powers of the President and legislature, as well as on the judiciary, by defining the legitimate function of each branch of the government; it also imposes a limit on the jurisdiction of law by the stipulation of definite rights which may not be legally annulled. To object that the Constitution can be interpreted according to the interest of the legislator is to concede the point; there is a legal document in existence which can be interpreted, indeed misinterpreted. From the fact however that fundamental laws can be misapplied, or disobeyed, or even ignored, it does not follow that the laws do not exist or, notwithstanding their lack of efficacy, do not have legal validity.

The recognition that law may exist independently of and prior to a given sovereign entails the fact that all laws need not be issued by the sovereign (or his delegated legislature). In fact, the initial designation of an individual or group as the legal sovereign, as distinct from 'sovereign' by force, requires the prior existence of laws of succession. Spinoza recognizes this point in his discussion of the fundamental laws of the dominion which define the organs of government, and in his implicit distinction between proper power and force.[27]

The sovereign then is not absolute in the sense of being above all legal restrictions — the laws of the sovereign must be validated

---

[26] Bodin (*De Republica Libra Sex*, Bk. I, Ch. 8); Hobbes (*Leviathan*, Part II, Chs. 18, 21); Ihering (*Law as a Means to an End*, Ch. 8, Sect. 9); and Austin (*The Province of Jurisprudence Determined*, Lecture VI) among others deny limitations to the power of the sovereign.

[27] It is believed that a more general recognition of the significance of this point would help clarify certain issues in international law. If it is acknowledged that there are in fact legal limits to the power of a sovereign within a state, the *prima facie* difficulties with the notion of legal control of sovereign states within the international community might be modified.

within the framework defined by the constitution, written or unwritten. Of course it is always possible for a given sovereign to deny the validity of the fundamental laws. Until a certain point such seditious acts would be considered illegal — beyond that point one speaks of a revolution (or a reorganization of government) which carries with it its new law. Whatever the terminology, the fact remains that there are legal limits to the power and jurisdiction of the sovereign although it is certainly true that such limits can be and often are usurped.

The fundamental laws of the state, as all laws, are expressed in general and often ambiguous terms allowing for a wide range of possible subsequent legislation. In order to delimit these ambiguous boundaries defining legality, other (moral) criteria have been introduced to determine the proper limits to sovereignty and law. This question of the proper or just limits to sovereignty and the proper or just jurisdiction of law introduces an evaluative element ultimately derived from one's notion of the function of law and of the legislator with respect to the place of both in the state. Implicit in such analysis is a theory of social ethics. For a legal theory to develop these issues it must acknowledge ethical standards independent of the criteria for legal validity. This procedure implies that the class of (legally) possible laws delimited by the fundamental laws is theoretically more inclusive than the class of proper laws. For example, the charge of unconstitutionality typically refers to social, ethical or political theories as the basis of the interpretation of the constitution of a state. It is contended that these are not inappropriate or *ad hoc* considerations — the real danger is the lack of awareness of their presence insofar as this allows the introduction of unanalyzed factors.

It is of interest to note that Spinoza distinguishes legal limits to sovereignty, determined by the fundamental laws; proper limits to sovereignty, determined by objective standards of justice; and NATURAL limits to sovereignty, determined by natural law. This scheme applies as well to Spinoza's notion of the sphere of legal jurisdiction.

The notion of natural limits to the sovereign's power and of the jurisdiction of law indicates limits implicit in the nature of things, independent of legal and moral strictures. This is the recognition, noted above, that there are certain commands which cannot be validated — not because they are 'illegal' or unjust — but because they cannot be enforced, they cannot be obeyed. It may be that this point carries the key to the supposed incommensurability of diverse legal systems; the common denominator, as it were, would be the generic traits of human nature which set pre-determined limits to possible legislation. If so, an adequate analysis of these generic traits would allow legal theory to advance a general theory of the nature and limits to sovereignty and the sphere of legal control which would also, of necessity, be applicable to actual legal systems. Such a scheme both recognizes and builds on the conception of law and legal institutions as natural 'entities' existing within the natural world.[28]

Spinoza's notion of an amoral natural law, or what has been termed the generic traits of human nature, makes it possible to analyze positive law within a framework which is not tinged with moralistic or teleologic absolutism. The power of a sovereign need not be associated with Divine right nor at the other extreme with arbitrary force; rather the power of any human individual, as well as the limits of that power, is explicable by reference to the nature of men as a species of natural beings existing in the natural universe. Such an analysis is capable of dealing with the dual nature of man as both the master of nature and as a part of nature — the recognition of this fundamental dialectic is perhaps the most important insight which Spinoza and other naturalists have adapted from ancient Greek philosophy.

F. THE PROBLEM OF THE END OF LAW AND OF THE DUTY OF THE SUBJECT AND THE SOVEREIGN

It is believed that the question of the end of law and of the duty or

---

[28] There is a certain resemblance between this position and Geny's theory of the universal factors or 'givens' (natural law) at the basis of positive law, although Geny considers postulates of justice as part of the natural law (whereas Spinoza's natural law is amoral). Cf. *Science et Technique en droit privé positif,* Part II, Sects. 166-170.

obligation of both subject and sovereign cannot be decided within the conceptual framework of a legal philosophy, although the determination of these issues is of basic importance in the construction of a philosophy of law. Nevertheless these questions must ultimately be referred to a prior analysis of the function and rationale of the state, the place of the citizens, the sovereign and civil law within the state. Within this framework legal philosophy can determine the way in which law can best fulfill its function and can determine the obligation of the subjects and the sovereign with respect to furthering this aim.

Depending on one's conception of the state — for example, the power state, the ideal state, the democratic state, the Rechtsstaat, the organic state, the nation state or the state as the City of God — the function and the instrumentality of law achieves a different significance. In the power state, for example, the primary function of law is taken to be the achievement of an order geared to the advantage of the lawmaking authority; whereas in the democratic state, one of the functions of law is to guarantee certain rights of individuals against infringement by authority. Clearly the notion of duty or obligation to the law also takes on significantly different meaning within the terms of these theories: in the power state the subjects have an absolute duty to obey the laws 'balanced' by the absolute power of the sovereign who, being above both his subjects and the law, is obliged to nothing; whereas in the democratic state, obligation takes on a quite different character.

With respect to the question of the function of law, it is possible to extract a minimal but significant agreement implicit in the diverse theories: the notion of some sort of regulation of human conduct. Law is seen to have the function of controlling and directing behavior within the state. It is possible that this point is tautological — certainly the diversity of types of regulation makes the point equivocal. Yet if this notion of regulation is considered more fully, particularly in its expanded meaning, namely, the regulating of human lives, certain points can be made. Spinoza's analysis of human nature and social institutions is at the basis of the scheme offered below.

There are certain minimal conditions which must be met if a legal system is to function efficaciously in regulating behavior: it must be possible to enforce a reasonable portion of the rules which are required by the plan envisaged. This requires sufficient power located in some designatable group or individual and a second group which allows itself to be subjected to that force (these groups may overlap). There are of course several reasons why human beings obey rules — from fear, from respect, from habit, or from hope of profit. Ultimately the first three must be absorbed by the fourth — it is in the final analysis impossible to coerce a man into acting against his understanding of his own advantage short of actual physical manipulation during which choice is temporarily annulled. Men are incapable of doing anything which they do not desire to do and they only desire those things which they imagine will lead to satisfaction and happiness.

Since sanctions are required in an order which attempts to control human behavior, it must be noted that the existence of sanctions and of an agency to apply the sanctions implies the prior existence of an actual legal order — if an order is not accepted as a legal order, infliction of punishment cannot function as a legal sanction. Actual imposition of evil cannot force a man to accept a system of rules as a legal code and unless he accepts the rules as legally binding, legal punishments, i.e., sanctions, cannot exist as such. In other words, a legal order or system cannot be based on brute force: there must at the very least be an acceptance of this force-pattern as legitimate, that is, as legally binding. Without this acceptance there are war and victors, but since there is no semblance of a legitimate legal order or legitimate authority there can be no sanctions or civil disobedience.[29] There are in short no rules which are not ACCEPTED as rules and if there are no rules one cannot speak of a legal system. Thus the notion that the function of law is the achievement of some kind of regulation of behavior implies that the code offered appeals to men as advantageous. This

---

[29] It is curious, with respect to this point, that writers, e.g., Kelsen, in arguing for the existence of international law, desirous of locating sanctions in the legal order, contend that war is a sanction. War on the contrary is not a sanction applied by a legal order but is indicative of the breakdown of that order.

does not entail that the system will necessarily be just (fair, equitable) — men have too much fear and too much stupidity for the stricture of appeal to guarantee a just system.

In addition, a plan offered as regulatory and efficacious must fulfill the formal requirement of a discernable system of application. This is usually expressed as the need to apply the law fairly, that is, when it is relevant. The possible moral injustice of this stricture was well noted by Anatole France in his penetrating remark, "The law in its majesty draws no distinction but forbids rich and poor alike from begging in the streets or from sleeping in the public parks". It is also necessary that a legal system contains no laws which contradict each other in their directive force unless other rules are supplied within the system that determine which rules take precedence. Similarly, in the simpler case of a game, if one indiscriminately applies the rules and introduces contradictory rules, one can no longer be said to be playing that game, but is rather playing a different game of making up rules and contradictions. Both of these formal conditions are implied by the notion of law functioning to regulate behavior.

Finally, a legal system should also include rules of succession which determine the eligible sovereign, either by appointment, or by hereditary or elective qualifications. This requirement, although implied by the notion of the desired continuity of the system, is not an absolute requirement insofar as it is possible, although extremely cumbersome, for a legal system to exist which did not account for its own continuance pending the termination of the legal control of its present sovereign. The result would be the breakdown of the legal order and the introduction of a new legal order when such an occasion arose. It might be that this sort of arrangement is characteristic of the situation in international law.

These conditions which are considered pre-requisite for the effective regulation of human behavior, taken as the end of a legal system, are compatible with diverse theories of the nature of law and of the state, and with diverse theories of the type of regulation desirable. These descriptive requirements cannot uniquely determine the social or ethical purpose of institutions; this ultimately requires evaluation with respect to conceptions of the proper mode of regulation or the proper 'plan of life'. A scheme which does not determine the ethical function of law and the state can do no more than offer a formal and abstract characterization of minimal requirements for the existence of a legal order. Ultimately the formal scheme must be interpreted as it were by an evaluation of the various types of regulation compatible with the general requirements for achievement of regulation. Even if this latter procedure is pejoratively labeled the introduction of ideals or ideologies this does not make it any less necessary.

The question of the duty of the subject and the sovereign requires a similar type of analysis, the key concept here being not regulation of behavior but right. Parallel to the fact that theories of the nature of law ultimately refer to some notion of regulation, theories of the obligation of the subjects and of the sovereign ultimately refer to some notion of right. Right may be characterized as legal, moral, natural, or Divine; it may be conceived as wholly on the side of the sovereign, or the subjects, or as shared by both; and it may be taken as absolute or relative, total or partial.

Spinoza's analysis of obligation offers some interesting observations which will be noted in lieu of a general treatment of this issue, which is too complex for adequate coverage in this discussion. The natural right (power) of the subjects limits the legal right of the sovereign by assigning limits to the commands which he can enforce. The obligation of the sovereign, construed as the absolute obligation not to do wrong, is comprised in the stricture not to attempt to impose commands which lead to the collapse of the state, that is, commands which cannot be obeyed. Such commands would be those which do not appeal to the multitude as advantageous and thus cannot achieve the efficacy necessary for validation. This point, as noted, ties up with the notion of natural rights and makes no reference to inalienable moral rights of subjects as human.

On the other hand, the subjects have no legal rights over and against the sovereign with respect to the sanctity of his law and the compelling force of its sanctions. The subject's absolute obligation to obey civil laws is explained by Spinoza in terms of the intrinsic value of the state with reference to the development of human nature and the fact that a stable state requires obedience to its dictates. This appears to be a very reasonable answer to the question, Why ought men, or Why ought I, obey the laws of the state, although it must be recognized that not all acts of disobedience have as their consequence the disruption of the state.[30]

According to Spinoza's analysis, subjects are obliged to obey all laws; that they might disapprove of some laws is irrelevant from the point of view of the integrity of the law and the authority of the state. The disparity between the rights and duties of the sovereign and the subjects is synthesized in the notion of the state as one mind — the notion of an ideal harmony of the will of all. This indeed is a fiction whose only justification is pragmatic.

With reference to Spinoza's notion of law as the primary instrument which the state uses to institute conditions conducive to the rational (moral) development of men, the sovereign can be said to have a moral obligation to institute rational (just) laws. This obligation is extra-legal insofar as non-fulfillment of the duty does not deprive a sovereign of legal power or rights. Analogous to this is the moral duty of the subject to develop a higher level of rationality. This would result in a more adequate understanding of his true advantage as tied up with the continuance and security of the civil state.

However, a citizen as subject is said to fulfill his obligation to the state if he obeys its laws, whatever the motivation, and a sovereign as legislator fulfills his obligation to the citizens if he maintains a secure and stable state, whether just or unjust. The notion of moral rights and of moral obligations cannot on principle be explicated by exclusive reference or reduction to legality or legal entities (subject and sovereign). This does not mean however that ethical concepts are irrelevant to an analysis of obligation to law; even though legality and morality refer to different dimensions, obligation can be construed as tied up with both levels.[31]

---

[30] Cf. Wasserstrom's paper, "Disobeying the Law", *J. of Phil*, 10/12/61 for a discussion of this point.
[31] Although Spinoza holds that one has a moral obligation to fulfill all legal obligations, this point, as contended in Chapter 4, is not substantiated by his analysis. Since valid laws are not necessarily just, the legal obligation to obey valid laws need not carry a moral obligation. If this is recognized, a theory can make sense out of the notion of the moral right, in fact, moral

G. CONCLUSION

In conclusion, it is suggested that the significance of Spinoza's position for the contemporary theorist lies more in his approach to the study of civil law than in the substantive details of his analysis. Certainly it would not be easy or particularly useful to find a philosopher willing to subscribe to Spinoza's metaphysics, although his ethical and political philosophy are closer to the contemporary naturalistic perspective. The approach indicated in his analysis however can be of philosophical use in structuring a legal theory with quite different content.

Spinoza based his analysis of civil law on his theory of human nature and its powers, which is placed within the wider context of the nature of social communities, their foundations and requirements for stability. Evaluative elements enter only indirectly, that is, in the analysis of the function of the state and of the function of law. Evaluation has reference to the fundamental ethical requirement of achieving (by means of, and within, the state) conditions requisite for the development of human power or virtue. Obligation and duty are analyzed within this framework and achieve a moral significance when coupled with the notion that the function of law and the state is to institute conditions within which men may achieve full moral development. Thus all endeavors which are related to the functioning of the state (and hence, by indirection, law) achieve in the final analysis a moral significance. Ethical judgment is refer-

---

obligation, to disobey unjust although valid laws. There is the danger implicit in those positions which absolutize the value of the state, e.g., Spinoza's understanding of the state as pre-requisite to moral emendation, that the moral rights of the individual will not be allowed effective protection. These last points are of course debatable in the sense that they assume a position with respect to the relative importance of individual rights as against the value of the state per se. Spinoza's point regarding the necessary existence of a stable state as prerequisite for the achievement of individual happiness complicates the issue without solving it. The existence of the state might be a necessary means for the development or delineation of conditions necessary for individual happiness taken as the end of just or proper human effort; but this indicates that the value of the state as means is subordinated to the ultimate value of the individual. One of the problems of political and legal philosophy is to determine more concretely this relation between means and ends.

red to an independently developed ethics of the type referred to as objective relativism.

Summarized below are what are taken to be the most significant insights of Spinoza expressed in terms of his avoidance of the 'errors' of previous (and subsequent) legal philosophers:

Spinoza offers a solid basis for the development of a legal theory which can make sense of the diverse types of relations between law and morality, avoiding the problems of the schemes which identify all law with good law and the schemes which disallow consideration of the relationship.

His ethical characterization of man based on a theory of human nature does not rest on a claim to discover the existence of intrinsic goodness in the scheme of the universe. Ultimately such an *a priori* claim would have had to rest on an absolutistic or idealistic conception of the intrinsic value of created beings. Nor does Spinoza jump to the extreme which denies all objective status to value judgments. He develops instead a conception of value or perfection by consideration of the essential or generic traits of human beings with respect to the development of human powers or virtues, ultimately the powers of freedom and rationality. This is a fundamentally naturalistic type of analysis which makes it possible to certify the meaningfulness of objective, albeit relative, value judgments. Civil law as a human institution can then be objectively evaluated in terms of its fulfillment of the conditions necessary for the achievement of human perfection, and legislation itself can be based on objective moral principles.

His notion of an amoral natural law releases him from the classical notion that positive law is derived by reason from a higher (moral) law. The higher law for Spinoza becomes the actual traits of the natural world — thus not a law at all but rather a scheme for recognizing the mode of operation of efficient causality and the generic traits of natural processes. His conception of natural rights (or powers) carries a naturalistic emphasis as against the more usual notion of the Divine sanctification of man derivative from a teleological view of the universe. This conception achieves significance in legal theory with respect to the question of the limits to sovereign power and the jurisdiction of law. Spinoza's notion of natural limits, i.e., the impossibility of infringing natural law, gives a realistic appraisal of the actual situation without reference to a moralistic or teleologic absolutism.

Spinoza's notion of the inter-relationship of will and reason allows him to take a stand between theories which hold reason as the source of law or will as the source of law. This position introduces internal criteria for judging the goodness of law based on an epistemological analysis of adequate and inadequate ideas.

His notion of obligation and of the end of law is developed through analysis of the desires of men and the possible modes of their achievement. He is able to avoid the incredible reduction of obligation to liability to sanctions and the questionable identification of obligation with subservience to the judiciary will of God, as well as indicating a set of natural conditions necessary for the achievement of an efficacious legal order.

Spinoza also mediates between those theories which focus change as essential to law and those which focus stability; the fundamental laws of the dominion guarantee a certain permanent core whereas change in circumstances and change in the level of ethical consciousness in the multitude assures and allows fluctuations in the content of law relative to developing notions of advantage.

Finally the conception of civil law as a tool of the state — the latter having moral aims, natural limits and legal jurisdiction — accomplishes a realistic appraisal of law as a natural institution with its own mode of functioning, its own limits, and its own excellence.

In conclusion, since the intention of this work was to extract, from an analysis of Spinoza's philosophy, a scheme for dealing with problems of legal theory, in partial justification of this endeavor it can be noted firstly, that Spinoza is one of the few major philosophers whose legal theory has been almost consistently ignored; secondly, that there is much that Spinoza's approach can teach contemporary jurisprudence with respect to the need for an analysis of civil law within the framework of a metaphysically grounded ethical and political philosophy; thirdly, that the general scheme extracted in this chapter from the analysis of Spinoza's theory in the first four chapters is believed to be sufficiently formalized to avoid requiring substantial agreement with principles of Spinoza's philosophy, particularly those points criticized in Chapter IV; and lastly, that contemporary jurisprudence is in need of some philosophical scheme.

APPENDIX A

NOTES ON THE CLASSICAL DOCTRINE OF NATURAL LAW

There is no single definition of the essence of natural law even if the attempt at definition is limited to the classical notion of natural law — that is, the natural law of the Greeks, Romans and Middle Ages. It is perhaps true to say that there are as many definitions or conceptions of natural law as there have been natural law theorists. The issues, then, will not be approached as an attempt to sum up the diverse positions into a neat formula but rather to indicate the key doctrines of the central figures in the development of natural law theory prior to Spinoza. Following this presentation, the question of the existence of any agreement among the doctrines will be studied. For the most part this will focus on the intention of natural law theory with respect to the problems which natural lawyers have attempted to solve within the framework of legal theory or philosophy of law. The final phrase distinguishes natural law theory from positivist theories which admit questions concerning standards of justice or good law but consider these issues as part of ethical theory rather than legal theory proper.

A. THE GREEK PERIOD

The relation between a divine law of nature and human laws was first expressed in the Western world by Heraclitus in the 5th century B. C. The universal immutable divine law is reason itself (*logos*), the order and destiny of the world, to which human law ought to conform. "For all human laws are nourished by one which is divine. For it governs as far as it will, and is sufficient for all, and more than enough." (Kathleen Freeman, *Ancilla to the Pre-Socratic Philosophers* (Oxford, Basil Blackwell, 1956), frag. 114). "Moderation is the greatest virtue, and wisdom is to speak the truth and to act according to nature, paying heed (thereto)." (Freeman, frag. 112).

For Plato, human law is a product of reason and is based on ideal laws; that is, law is discovered, not invented. The aim of law is to lead men to virtue, peace and happiness. All laws must be in harmony with justice which is the immutable unwritten law discoverable through reason. Plato suggests that law is of divine origin and has a distinct moral value. "There is one among these cords which every man ought to grasp and never let go, but to pull with it against all the rest; and this is the sacred and golden cord of reason, called by us the common law of the state." (*Laws,* in *The Dialogues of Plato,* trans. B. Jowett, Vol. II (New York, Random House, 1937), Bk. I (645).) "A state ought to be free and wise and harmonious, and that a legislator ought to legislate with a view to this end." (*Laws,* Bk. III, (693).) "If states are to be named after their rulers, the true state ought to be called by the name of the God who rules over wise men." (*Laws,* Bk. IV (713).) "The state in which the law is above the rulers, and the rulers are the inferiors of the law, has salvation, and every blessing which the Gods can confer." (*Laws,* Bk. IV (715).)

For Aristotle, the universal or common law is also the rule of reason rather than desire. Laws which are according to nature and natural justice, as distinct from particular law and legal justice, are binding on all men and ought to be followed in civil legislation (particular laws). Civil law ought to be directed to the good of men as the concrete expression of the moral ideal, the rational life of man in the state. Civil law ought to aim at embodying justice with respect to the various and changing circumstances of civil relationships in the state. "He who bids the law rule may be deemed to bid God and Reason alone rule, but he who bids man rule adds an element of the beast; for desire is a wild beast, and passion perverts the minds of rulers, even when they are the best of men. The law is reason unaffected by desire." (*Politics* in *The Student's Oxford Aristotle,* trans. W. D. Ross (London, Oxford University Press,

1942), Vol. VI, Bk. III, 1287a 28.) "Law, now, I understand, to be either peculiar or universal; peculiar, to be that which has been marked out by each people in reference to itself, and that this is partly unwritten, partly written. I call that law universal, which is conformable merely to the dictates of nature." (*Aristotle's Treatise on Rhetoric,* trans. Theodore Buckley (London, Geo. Bell & Sons, 1883), Bk. I, ch. 13, 1373b 4.) "If the written law be opposed to his case, he must avail himself of the universal law, and of topics of equity, as more absolutely just; ... equity remains for ever, and varies not at any time, neither does the universal law, for this is in conformity to nature; but that the written law does frequently vary." (*Rhetoric,* Bk. I, ch. 15, 1375a 27). "Of political justice part is natural, part legal, — natural, that which everywhere has the same force and does not exist by people's thinking this or that; legal, that which is originally indifferent, but when it has been laid down is not indifferent..." (*Ethics,* in *The Student's Oxford Aristotle,* trans. W. D. Ross (London, Oxford University Press, 1942), Vol. V, Bk. V, ch. 7, 1134b 18).

The Stoic philosophers, denying the class distinctions found in Plato and Aristotle, considered all men as equal and mankind as one community of rational beings. This consideration led to a focus on reason as inherent in Nature and right reason was identified with the law of Nature. Thus the man who lives according to reason lives both naturally and morally. The natural law is a universal moral law applicable to all men, whether Greeks or barbarians, free men or slaves. "Law is the ruler of all things divine and human, the settled arbiter of good and evil, the guide to justice and injustice, the sovereign and lord of all who are by nature social animals. It directs what must be done and forbids the opposite." (Chrysippus, quoted in Cairns, p. 127.) "Law is highest reason, imbedded in nature, which commands what should be done, and forbids the contrary." (Quoted by Cicero in *De legibus* 1.6, from Chrysippus, in Friedrich, p. 29). "The common law, going through all things, which is the same with Zeus who administers the whole universe." (Quoted by Diogenes Laertius from Chrysippus, in Pound, *Outlines of Lectures on Jurisprudence,* p. 61.)

B. THE ROMAN PERIOD

Mankind, according to Cicero, following the Stoics, is a universal community; thus the unwritten natural law, based on the common nature of men, is universal, and as issuing from God is eternal and immutable. Divine reason gives this supreme law of justice to man which teaches human equality as its first principle. Cicero, as the natural law theorists before him, contrasted the natural law with human law, the contrast of nature with convention, and held that the *jus naturale* measured the validity of positive law. Human laws should be framed according to the eternal universal law of nature, taken as a standard for judging the justice and rationality of a law. "True law is right reason conformable to nature, universal, unchangeable, eternal, whose commands urge us to duty, and whose prohibitions restrain us from evil. This law cannot be contradicted by any other law, and is not liable either to derogation or abrogation. Neither the senate nor the people can give us any dispensation for not obeying this universal law of justice. It needs no other expositor and interpreter than our own conscience. It is not one thing at Rome, and another at Athens; one thing today, and another tomorrow; but in all times and nations this universal law must for ever reign, eternal and imperishable. It is the sovereign master and emperor of all beings. God himself is its author, its promulgator, its enforcer." (Cicero, *On the Commonwealth,* Bk. Bk. III, 22, 13.)

Although it is difficult to find substantial agreement concerning the nature of the natural law among the writers of the *Corpus Juris* of Justinian (534 A.D.), several points can be made. The simplest classification of laws into *Jus Civile* (Roman law) and *Jus Gentium* (law common to all nations) was altered by the introduction of the Greek theory of the natural law, the *Jus Naturale*. The *Jus Naturale* was at times identified with the *Jus Gentium* and at times distinguished from it as the ideal law to which actual law and custom ought to approximate. It was never asserted however that positive law is invalidated if it goes against the rational ideal law of nature. Although the distinction between the natural and the conventional was fundamental, the former was taken only as a guide or an ideal standard of justice and equity, which is never fully realized in positive law.[1]

C. ST. AUGUSTINE

Although Augustine stressed the ability of human reason, independent of revelation, to attain knowledge of the good, he also stressed the real distinction between the terrestial world and the Kingdom of God. Although the true City of God exists in heaven it is represented on earth by the community of the faithful.

Justice, in Augustine's conception, entails giving to everyone his own and above all giving to God His own, i.e., piety and worship. The function of the political order is to maintain peace, subject to the decision of the higher community represented by the church, which determines the justice of a particular government.

Positive law (*lex temporalis*) relates to the temporal world and punishes breaches of the peace determined by the rule of the given order. Positive law does not function as a moral law which leads men to salvation. The eternal law of God (*lex aeterna*) rules the eternal order and functions to make men good. However there is a significant relationship between the two legal orders: the eternal law, directed toward the Christian virtues, determines the limits of positive law. Positive law may not transgress eternal law if it is to have the force of law: "that which is not just seems to be no law at all" (*De libero arbitrio,* i, 5). Thus positive law must embody justice as determined by the eternal law if it is to be valid.[2]

D. THE MIDDLE AGES

The Decretum of Gratian (cir. 1140 A.D.) formulated the canon law conception of the natural law. The *jus naturale* is of Divine

[1] Paton, George W., *A Text-book of Jurisprudence* (Oxford, Clarendon Press, 1951), pp. 80-81; and Jolowicz, H. F., *Historical Introduction to the Study of Roman Law* (Cambridge, University Press, 1932), pp. 100-105 (Chap. VI).
[2] cf. Carl Friedrich, *The Philosophy of Law in Historical Perspective* (Chicago, The University of Chicago Press, 1958), pp. 35-41 (Chap. V).

origin, an immutable eternal moral law given by God to man. Its precepts are confirmed by Revelation. The law is of human nature, alike in all man, and prevails over human law, written or unwritten. If human law contradicts natural law it cannot be considered valid.[3] Natural law "came into existence with the very creation of man as a rational being, nor does it vary in time but remains unchangeable". (*Decr. Grat.*, quoted in d'Entreves, p. 34). "Natural law absolutely prevails in dignity over customs and constitutions. Whatever has been recognized by usage, or laid down in writing, if it contradicts natural law, must be considered null and void." (*Decr. Grat.*, quoted in d'Entreves, p. 34).

Aquinas held that the natural law is man's participation through natural reason in the eternal law (the Divine reason governing the universe as the first cause). The *lex naturalis* is that part of the eternal law which is applicable to man, known through knowledge of human nature (not through faith which reveals Divine law). The natural law contains precepts ordering man to do good and avoid evil, but not all virtuous acts are prescribed by the natural law. The general principles of the natural law are immutable and universal whereas deductions from these principles may very according to circumstance, either by 'addition' or 'subtraction'. Human laws must conform to the natural law to be valid, that is, they must be ordered to the common good, although under certain circumstances prudence may direct one to obey unjust commands at the risk of public disturbance. For Aquinas natural law is both the foundation of morality and of political institutions and the standard by which they are judged. These principles are independent of revelation and can be known through natural reason. The following quotations are from the *Summa Theologica,* Part I of the Second Part, "Treatise on Law": "The natural law is nothing else than the rational creature's participation of the eternal law." (Ques. 91, Art. 2.) "This is the first precept of law, that good is to be pursued and done, and evil is to be avoided. All other precepts of the natural

---

[3] d'Entreves, Passerin, *Natural Law* (London, Hutchinson's University Library, 1951), pp. 33-36 (Chap. II).

law are based upon this, so that whatever the practical reason naturally apprehends as man's good belongs to the precepts of the natural law as something to be done or avoided." (Q. 94, Art. 2). "Every human law has just so much of the character of law as it is derived from the law of nature. But if in any point it differs from the law of nature, it is no longer a law but a corruption of law ... Something may be derived from the natural law in two ways: first, as a conclusion from premises, secondly, by way of determination of certain generalities." (Q. 95, Art. 2).

The Late Scholastics — Vittoria, Bellarmine, Suarez, Vasquez and De Soto — reasserted the idea of natural law against the previous critiques of William of Occam and the Reformers by a return to and elaboration of Aquinas' doctrines. The natural law is eternal and immutable and must be clearly distinguished from the *Jus Gentium* which is a product of human convention, albeit common to all civilized nations. These doctrines of the law of nature and the law of nations were developed with respect to current problems, particularly the question of the relation between pagan and Christian states and the Divine right theory of kings. The Late Scholastics developed a theory of the state as an institution of the natural law, necessary for the development of human nature. It was held that since the state is formed by an original covenant of the people, political authority comes immediately from the people, although in the final analysis all power is derived from God. By natural law the government is bound to serve the common good and if it falls short the people have a natural right to resist. Liberty belongs to the natural law, it is a natural right since by nature all men are free and equal. The right to property is also conceived as a natural right.[4] The focus on natural rights in this period introduced a new emphasis in natural law theory which, in its historical development, led to the revolutionary doctrine of the inalienable rights of man as individual as against the earlier concept of the natural ordering of man within the state. "Only that which is a measure of rectitude,

---

[4] Rommen, Heinrich A., "The Natural Law in the Renaissance Period" in *Natural Law Institute Proceedings,* Vol. II, edited by A. L. Scanlan (Notre Dame, Indiana, College of Law, University of Notre Dame, 1949), pp. 98-105.

... only that which is a right and virtuous rule, can be called law." (This and the following quotations are from Francisco Suarez, *De Legibus ac Deo Legislatore,* quoted in Brown, *The Natural Law Reader,* pp. 95-96.) "The eternal law has first place, on account of its dignity and excellence, and because it is the source and origin of all laws." "The natural law is made known to men in a twofold way, first through natural reason, and secondly, through the law of the Decalogue written on the Mosaic tablets."

Grotius' notion of the natural law continued the tradition of the Late Scholastics to a certain extent. The natural law is discoverable by men through reason, either *a priori,* through analysis of the rational and social nature of man, or *a posteriori* by examining principles accepted by all nations. He stresses the self-evidence and clarity of the principles and emphasizes their immutability by noting that they could not even be abolished by God. That is, in contrast to the Scholastics, he maintained that natural laws are independent of divine command. He gave the natural law theory a secular basis in the rational and social nature of men, who are held to desire peaceful life in society, a notion traceable to the Stoics. "And this tendency to the conservation of society . . . is the source of *Jus,* or Natural Law, properly so called." (This and the following quotations are from Hugo Grotius, *De Jure Belli et Pacis,* Vol. I, Prolegomena, Sec. 8). "Natural Law is the Dictate of Right Reason, indicating that any act, from its agreement or disagreement with the rational (and social) nature (of man) has in it a moral turpitude or a moral necessity; and consequently that such act is forbidden or commanded by God, the author of nature." (Vol. I, Ch. I, X.) "Natural Law is so immutable that it cannot be changed by God himself." (Vol. I, Ch. I, X).

The last figure to be considered is Hobbes whose theory of natural law was in fact not a theory of natural law but of natural rights. Hobbes is not considered in this classification as a classical natural law theorist although he does indeed acknowledge the authority of the immutable natural law. However, according to Hobbes these laws have no binding power in themselves insofar as they lack sanctions. Thus they are not considered as laws proper since law (lex) binds one to obedience, i.e., is dependent upon sanctions. All actual law, then, is civil law which is commanded and sanctioned by the sovereign to whom the natural rights (*jus*) of the citizens have been transferred. The natural right which is left to the individual, that is, the liberty of action, is contained in those things which have not been denied by civil law. The laws of nature teach men how to achieve peace in the state and preserve their own lives — a code of prudential rules of conduct — but not being sanctioned they are not properly called laws. "Reason suggests convenient articles of peace, upon which men may be drawn to agreement. These articles are they which otherwise are called the Laws of Nature . . ." (This and the following quotations are from Hobbes, *Leviathan,* ch. 13). "A Law of Nature, *lex naturalis,* is a precept or general rule, found out by reason, by which a man is forbidden to do that which is destructive of his life or takes away the means of preserving the same and to omit that by which he thinks it may be best preserved." (ch. 14). "These dictates of reason men used to call by the name of laws, but improperly, for they are but conclusions or theorems concerning what conduces to the conservation and defense of themselves, whereas law, properly, is the word of him that by right has command over others." (ch. 15).

It is of interest, at this point, to determine the similarities of formulation or intention in the natural law theories outlined above, with the exception of Hobbes. First it can be said that the very conception of natural law requires a two-fold recognition: on the one hand the primitive identification of all law with divine law must be overcome, and on the other hand, the identification of all law with positive or human law must be avoided — in other words, one must recognize that all law is not immutable and universal, nor is all law mutable and particular. The classical natural law theorists were interested in determining the absolute (immutable) law which changing (human) law could approach as its model or exemplar. Not all the theorists took the next step of declaring human law invalid if contrary to the higher natural law, but they all recognize the natural law as the standard for judging the goodness or badness of human law. This point ties up with a further intention prevalent in natural law theory throughout its history: the attempt to ground the authority of law on reason rather than will, and to ground the existence and function of the state and of law on nature rather than expediency. Underlying these points is the conviction that the denial of reason and nature would leave no recourse to institutions based on arbitrary and unlimited power disguised under the formula that might is right. In other words, the natural lawyer has been concerned to maintain that a relation between the legal and the just is grounded in the nature of the universe, and can be discovered through natural reason. Natural law theory asserts that law is a part of ethics.

It is possible to indicate certain basic beliefs or assumptions underlying natural law theory: (1) the notion of an ordered universe governed by reason, either divine or natural; (2) the notion of men sharing a common nature as rational beings whose intellect is capable of discovering the eternal order; (3) the notion of natural justice or a moral law implicit in the natural order.

In addition to these assumptions of natural law theory, the common assertions of classical natural law theory can be summarized as follows: (1) the natural law is an immutable objective moral law applicable to human behavior in the natural world; (2) human law ought to recognize and embody the natural law; (3) the justice or goodness of positive law, if not its validity, is determined by its coincidence with natural law; (4) natural law can guide legislators in framing laws for changing circumstances by offering standards of judgment applicable to changing social facts; and (5) the belief common to natural law theories that a theory of positive law must deal with the question of moral standards applicable to human law. This last point is not merely systematic but indicates the belief that positive law in its essence is not amoral, and thus cannot be adequately understood without reference to the objective criteria of goodness and badness outlined by the natural law.

APPENDIX B

LATIN QUOTATIONS FROM SPINOZA

Introduction

1. Legis nomen absolute sumptum significat id, secundum quod unumquodque individuum, vel omnia vel aliquot ejusdem speciei una, eademque certa ac determinata ratione agunt; ea vero vel a necessitate naturae, vel ab hominum placito dependet. Gebhardt, Vol. III, p. 57, 1. 23-27.

3. (Lex) ... ab hominum placito autem, & quae magis proprie jus appellatur, est ea, quam homines ad tutius, & commodius vivendum, vel ob alias causas, sibi & aliis praescribunt. G. Vol. III, p. 57, 1. 28-31.

4. Verum enimvero quoniam nomen legis per translationem ad res naturales applicatum videtur, & communiter per legem nihil aliud intelligitur, quam mandatum, quod homines & perficere, & negligere possunt. G. Vol. III, p. 58, 1. 28-31.

5. ideo Lex particularius definienda videtur, nempe, quod sit ratio vivendi, quam homo sibi, vel aliis ob aliquem finem praescribit. G. Vol. III, p. 58, 1. 33-35.

Chapter I

3. unde factum est, ut pro lege maxime haberetur ratio vivendi, quae hominibus ex aliorum imperio praescribitur. G. Vol. III, p. 59, 1. 8-10.

10. Frustra enim subdito imperaret, ut illum odio habeat, qui eum sibi beneficio junxit, ut amet, qui ei damnum intulit, ut contumeliis non offendatur, ut a metu liberari non cupiat, & alia perplurima hujusmodi, quae ex legibus humanae naturae necessario sequuntur. G. Vol. III, p. 201, 1. 17-21.

11. Plures sane, & acerbiores contentiones inter parentes, & liberos, quam inter dominos, & servos moveri solent, nec tamen Oeconomiae interest Jus paternum in dominium mutare, & liberos perinde, ac servos habere. G. Vol. III, p. 298, 1. 20-23.

17. status civilis naturaliter instituitur ad metum communem adimendum, & communes miserias propellendum, ac proinde id maxime intendit, quod unusquisque, qui ratione ducitur, in statu naturali conaretur, sed frustra. G. Vol. III, p. 286, 1. 26-29.

26. non enim ratio obtemperandi, sed obtemperantia subditum facit. G. Vol. III, p. 202, 1. 2-3.

27. Quapropter raro admodum contingere potest, ut summae potestates absurdissima imperent; ipsis enim maxime incumbit, ut sibi prospiciant, & imperium retineant, communi bono consulere, & omnia ex rationis dictamine dirigere. G. Vol. III, p. 194, 1. 12-15.

29. sed quia universalis potentia totius naturae nihil est praeter potentiam omnium individuorum simul. G. Vol. III, p. 189, 1. 21-23.

34. Jura belli uniuscujusque Civitatis esse; pacis autem non unius, sed duarum ad minimum Civitatum esse Jura. G. Vol. III, p. 290, 1. 7-8.

Chapter II

3. (Legem). per divinam autem, quae solum summum bonum, hoc

est, Dei veram cognitionem, & amorem spectat. G. Vol. III, p. 59, 1. 25-26.

4. Legis nomen absolute sumptum significat id, secundum quod unumquodque individuum, vel omnia vel aliquot ejusdem speciei una, eademque certa ac determinata ratione agunt; ea vero vel a necessitate naturae, vel ab hominum placito dependet. G. Vol. III, p. 57, 1. 23-27.

7. Unde sequitur, Dei affirmationes & negationes aeternam semper necessitatem sive veritatem involvere. G. Vol. III, p. 63, 1. 10-12.

8. cum tamen haec omnia solius humanae naturae sint attributa, & a natura divina prorsus removenda. G. Vol. III, p. 64, 1. 13-15.

12. tum quia sine Deo nihil esse, neque concipi potest, tum etiam, quia de omnibus dubitare possumus, quam diu Dei nullam claram, & distinctam habemus ideam. G. Vol. III, p. 59-60, 1. 34-1.

21. Sic etiam jussum de non committendo adulterio, solius rei publicae & imperii utilitatem respicit; nam si documentum morale docere voluisset, quod non solam reipublicae utilitatem, sed animi tranquillitatem, & veram uniuscujusque beatitudinem respiceret, tum non tantum actionem externam, sed & ipsum animi consensum damnaret. G. Vol. III, p. 70, 1. 26-31.

23. hoc est, actiones, quae in se indifferentes sunt, & solo instituto bonae vocantur, vel, quae aliquod bonum ad salutem necessarium repraesentant. G. Vol. III, p. 62, 1. 6-8.

30. quia res per proximas suas causas definire, & explicare debemus. G. Vol. III, p. 58, 1. 19-20.

39. unicuique Civitati jus integrum est solvendi foedus, quandocunque vult. G. Vol. III, p. 290, 1. 14-15.

44. Per jus & institutum naturae nihil aliud intelligo, quam regulas

naturae uniuscujusque individui, secundum quas unumquodque naturaliter determinatum concipimus ad certo modo existendum & operandum. G. Vol. III, p. 189, 1. 12-15.

45. sed quia universalis potentia totius naturae nihil est praeter potentiam omnium individuorum simul, hinc sequitur unumquodque individuum jus summum habere ad omnia, quae potest. G. Vol. III, p. 189, 1. 21-24.

46. Et quia les summa naturae est, ut unaquaeque res in suo statu, quantum in se est, conetur perseverare, idque nulla alterius, sed tantum sui habita ratione, hinc sequitur unumquodque individuum jus summum ad hoc habere, hoc est (uti dixi), ad existendum & operandum prout naturaliter determinatum est. G. Vol. III, p. 189, 1. 25-30.

50. Quare concedendum unumquemque multa sibi sui juris reservare, quae propterea a nullius decreto, sed a suo solo pendent. G. Vol. III, p. 201, 1. 30-31.

Chapter III

3. cum tamen id, quod ratio malum esse dictat, non malum sit respectu ordinis, & legum universae naturae, sed tantum solius nostrae naturae legum respectu. G. Vol. III, p. 279, 1. 33-36.

14. atque adeo hominem eatenus liberum omnino voco, quatenus ratione ducitur, quia eatenus ex causis, quae per solam ejus naturam possunt adaequate intelligi, ad agendum determinatur, tametsi ex iis necessario ad agendum determinetur. G. Vol. III, p. 280, 1. 21-24.

Chapter IV

12. quippe nemo jus suum naturale, sive facultatem suam libere

ratiocinandi, & de rebus quibuscunque judicandi, in alium transferre, neque ad id cogi potest. G. Vol. III, p. 239, 1. 10-12.

13. Qui enim omnibus Civitatis mandatis obtemperare constituit, sive ejus potentiam metuit, vel quia tranquillitatem amat, is profecto suae securitati, saeque utilitati ex suo ingenio consulit. G. Vol. III, p. 285, 1. 28-31.

15. Quod imperii conservatio praecipue pendeat a subditorum fide, eorumque virtute & animi constantia in exequendis mandatis, ratio, & experientia quam clarissime docent. G. Vol. III, p. 203, 1. 12-14

17. adoeque impium etiam est, ex suo arbitrio aliquid contra decretum summae potestatis, cujus subditus est, facere, quandoquidem, si hoc unicuique liceret, imperii ruina inde necessario sequeretur. G. Vol. III, p. 242, 1. 6-9.

18. Quinimo nihil contra decretum, & dictamen propriae rationis agere potest, quamdiu juxta decreta summae potestatis agit; ipsa enim ratione suadente omnino decrevit, jus suum vivendi ex proprio suo judicio, in eandem transferre. G. Vol. III, p. 242, 1. 9-13.

20. at Jura civilia pendent a solo Civitatis decreto, atque haec nemini, nisi sibi, ut scilicet libera maneat, morem gerere tenetur, nec aliud bonum, aut malum habere, nisi quod ipsa sibi bonum, aut malum esse decernit. G. Vol. III, p. 294, 1. 6-9.

23. Atque adeo is, qui imperium tenet, nulla etiam alia de causa hujus contractus conditiones servare tenetur, quam homo in statu naturali, ne sibi hostis sit, tenetur cavere, ne se ipsum interficiat. G. Vol. III, p. 294, 1. 26-29.

25. ex his duobus, legibus scilicet & moribus, tantum oriri potest, quod unaquaeque natio singulare habeat ingenium, singularem conditionem & denique singularia praejudicia. G. Vol. III, p.217, 1. 21-24.

28. nam Christus, uti dixi, non ad imperium conservandum, & leges instituendum, sed ad solam legem universalem docendum missus fuit; & hinc facile intelligimus, Christum legem Mosis minime abrogavisse, quandoquidem Christus nullas novas leges in rempublicam introducere voluerit, nec aliud magis curaverit, quam documenta moralia docere, eaque a legibus Reipublicae distinguere. G. Vol. III, p. 70-71, 1. 33-5.

30. Nec unquam hominibus otiosis ingenium deest ad eludenda jura, quae instituuntur de rebus, quae absolute prohiberi nequeunt, ut sunt convivia, ludi, ornatus, & alia hujusmodi, quorum tantummodo excessus malus, & ex uniuscujusque fortuna aestimandus est, ita ut lege nulla universali determinari queat. G. Vol. III, p. 355, 1. 29-33.

34. At cum solius summae potestatis officium sit, determinare, quid saluti totius populi, & imperii securitati necesse sit, & quid necesse esse judicaverit, imperare, hinc sequitur, solius etiam summae potestatis officium esse, determinare, qua ratione unusquisque debet proximum pietate colere,hoc est, qua ratione unusquisque Deo obedire tenetur. G. Vol. III, p. 232, 1. 23-28.

SELECTED BIBLIOGRAPHY

WORKS BY SPINOZA

Spinoza, *Renati des Cartes Principiorum Philosophiae,* Pars I & II, *Cogitata Metaphysics* (Amsterdam, 1663).
——, *Principles of Descartes Philosophy,* trans. H. H. Britan (Chicago, Open Court Publishing Co.).
——, *Tractatus Theologico-Politicus* (Hamburg, Henricus Kunraht, 1670).
——, B.d.S. *Opera posthuma (Tractatus Politicus; Ethica; Tractatus de Intellectus Emendatione; Epistolae; Hebrew Grammar)* (Amsterdam, J. Rievwertsz, 1677).
——, *Works of Spinoza: Political Treatise; Theological Political Treatise,* Vol. I, trans. R. H. M. Elwes (New York, Dover Publications, Inc. 1951).
——, *Benedict de Spinoza, The Political Works,* trans. A. G. Wernham (Oxford, Clarendon Press, 1958).
——, *Ethics; On the Improvement of the Understanding,* ed. J. Gutmann (New York, Hafner Publishing Co., 1957).
——, *The Correspondence of Spinoza,* ed. A. Wolf (New York, Dial Press, 1927).
——, *Short Treatise on God, Man and His Well-Being (Korte Verhandeling van God, de Mensch, en deszelfs Welstand); Life of Spinoza,* trans. A. Wolf (London, Adam & Charles Black, 1910).
——, *Spinoza Opera,* ed. Carl Gebhardt (Heidelberg, C. Winter, 1925). Vol. I: *Korte Verhandeling van God, de Mensch, en deszelfs Welstand; Renati des Cartes Principiorum Philosophiae, Pars I & II; Cogitata Metaphysica; Compendium Grammatices Linguae Hebraeae.* Vol. II: *Tractatus de Intellectus Emendatione; Ethica.* Vol. III: *Tractatus Theologico-Politicus with Adnotationes; Tractatus Politicus.* Vol. IV: *Epistolae; Stelkonstige Reeckening van den Regenboog, Reeckening van Kanssen.*

BIBLIOGRAPHIES

The Oko-Gebhardt Collection, *Special Collections* (Columbia University Library).

New York Public Library, *List of Books Relating to Philosophy* (New York, 1908).
McKeon, Richard, *The Philosophy of Spinoza* (New York, Longmans, Green & Co., 1928), pp. 319-337.

WORKS ABOUT SPINOZA

Boasson, J. J., *De Rechtsidee en de Vrijheidsidee bij Spinoza* (Leiden, E. J. Brill, 1949).
Brasch, Moritz, *Benedict von Spinoza's System der Philosophie* (Berlin, Albert Wruck, 1870).
Broad, C. D., *Five Types of Ethical Theory* (New York, Harcourt Brace & Co., 1930), Section on Spinoza, pp. 15-52.
Brunschvicg, Leon, *Spinoza et Ses Contemporains* (Paris, Librairie Felix Alcan, 1923).
Caird, John, *Spinoza* (Edinburgh, William Blackwood & Sons, 1899).
Cairns, Huntington, *Legal Philosophy from Plato to Hegel* (Baltimore, John Hopkins Press, 1949), (Includes a chapter on Spinoza).
Carp, J. H., "Naturrecht und Pflichtbegriff nach Spinoza", *Chronicon Spinozanum,* Vol. I (1921), 81-90.
Coert, J., *Spinoza en Grotius* (Leiden, E. J. Brill, 1936).
Cohen, Morris R., "Spinoza: Prophet of Liberalism", *The New Republic* (March 30, 1927), 164-166.
Dessauer, Moritz, *Spinoza und Hobbes* (Breslau, Schletter'sche Buchhandlung, 1868).
Duff, Robert A., *Spinoza's Political and Ethical Philosophy* (Glasgow, James Maclehose & Sons, 1903).
Dunham, James, *Freedom and Purpose: An Interpretation of the Psychology of Spinoza* (Princeton, N.J., Princeton University Press, 1916).
Dunin-Borkowski, Stanislaus, *Der junge De Spinoza* (Münster, Aschendorffsche Buchhandlung, 1910).
Dunner, Joseph, *Baruch Spinoza and Western Democracy* (New York, Philosophical Library, 1955).
Eckstein, Walter, "Rousseau and Spinoza: Their Political Theories and Their Conception of Ethical Freedom", *Journal of the History of Ideas,* Vol. 5, No. 3 (6/44), 259-291.
Freudenthal, J., *Die Lebensgeschichte Spinoza's* (Leipzig, Veit & Co., 1899).
Gebhardt, Carl, *Spinoza als Politiker* (Heidelberg, C. Winter, 1908).
Gibson, James, "Spinoza's Political and Ethical Philosophy", *Ethics,* Vol. 14 (1903-1904).
Green, Thomas H., *Lectures on the Principles of Political Obligation* (London, Longmans, Green & Co., 1895), (Section on Spinoza, pp. 49-59).
Hallett, H. F., *Aeternitas: A Spinozistic Study* (Oxford, Clarendon Press, 1930).
——, *Benedict de Spinoza: The Elements of His Philosophy* (University of London, The Athlone Press, 1957).
Hoff, Josef, *Die Staatslehre Spinoza's* (Berlin, S. Calvary & Co., 1895).
Horn, J. E., *Spinoza's Staatslehre* (Dresden, Louis Ehlermann, 1863).

Husik, Isaac, "Studies on Spinoza", *Jewish Quarterly Review*, Vol. 19, No. 3, (1/29).
Janet, Paul, *Histoire de la Philosophie Morale et Politique*, Vol. II (Paris, Librarie Philosophique de Ladrange, 1858).
Joachim, Harold, *Spinoza's Tractatus de Intellectus Emendatione* (Oxford, Clarendon Press, 1940).
———, *A Study of the Ethics of Spinoza* (Oxford, Clarendon Press, 1941).
Kline, George L., "Spinoza: Six Recent Studies", *Journal of Philosophy*, Vol. 58 (6/22/61), 346-55.
Kriegsmann, Georg, *Die Rechts- und Staatstheorie des Benedict von Spinoza* (Wandsbeck, Fr. Puvogel, 1878).
Kroeger, A. E., "Spinoza", *Journal of Speculative Philosophy*, Vol. 9, No. 3 (7/75) 363-393.
Lauterpacht, H., "Spinoza and International Law", *British Year Book of International Law*, Vol. 8 (1927), 89-107.
Martineau, James, *A Study of Spinoza* (London, Macmillan & Co., 1895).
———, *Types of Ethical Theory*, Vol. I (Oxford, Clarendon Press, 1886), (Section on Spinoza, pp. 247-393).
McKeon, Richard, *The Philosophy of Spinoza* (New York, Longmans, Green & Co., 1928).
———, "Spinoza and Medieval Philosophy", *The Open Court*, Vol. 42, No. 3 (3/28), 129-145.
Menzel, Adolph, *Wandlungen in der Staatslehre Spinoza's* (Stuttgart, J. G. Cotta'sche Buchhandlung, 1898).
Meijer, Willem, "Over de beteekenis en de Waarde van het Godgeleerd Staatkundig Vertoog van B. Despinoza", *Tijdschrift voor wijsbegeerte*, Vol. 11, No. 4 (10/17), 467-483.
———, *Wat is de Staat? (naar Spinoza)* (The Hague, 1914).
Otto, Eduard, *Zur Beurteilung und Würdigung der Staatslehre Spinozas* (Darmstadt, Winter'sche Buchdruckerei, 1897).
Pollock, Sir Frederick, "Spinoza et le Machiavelisme", *La Revue Politique Internationale*, No. 36 (Jan.-June 1919), 1-11.
———, *Spinoza: His Life and Philosophy* (London, The Camelot Press, 1935).
Zac, Sylvain, *La Morale de Spinoza* (Paris, Presses Universitaires de France, 1959).

WORKS ON LEGAL THEORY

Aristotle, *The Student's Oxford Aristotle*, trans. W. D. Ross (London, Oxford University Press, 1942).
———, *Aristotle's Treatise on Rhetoric*, trans. T. Buckley (London, Geo. Bell & Sons, 1883).
Augustine, *De libero arbitrio*, trans. F. E. Tourscher (Philadelphia, Peter Reilly Co., 1937).
Austin, John, *Lectures on Jurisprudence* (London, John Murrary, 1873) (first published 1863).
Bodin, Jean, *De republica in Apologie de Rene Herpin pour la Republique de I. Bodin* (Geneva, G. Cartier, 1599) (first published 1576).

Briggs, Herbert, "Towards the Rule of Law", *American Journal of International Law,* Vol. 51 (1957), 517.
Brown, Brendan, *The Natural Law Reader* (New York, Oceana Publication, 1960).
Cardozo, Benjamin, *The Growth of the Law* (New Haven, Yale University Press, 1924).
——, *The Nature of the Judicial Process* (New Haven, Yale University Press, 1921).
——, *The Paradoxes of Legal Science* (New York, Columbia University Press, 1935).
Carritt, E. F., *Morals and Politics* (Oxford, Clarendon Press, 1935).
Cicero, *On the Commonwealth. On the Laws* (London, Bohn's Classical Library, 1853).
Cohen, Felix, *Ethical Systems and Legal Ideals* (New York, Falcon Press, 1933).
Cohen, Morris R., *Law and the Social Order* (New York, Harcourt, Brace & Co., 1933).
——, *Reason and Law* (New York, Collier Books, 1961).
——, *Reason and Nature* (Glencoe, Ill., Free Press, 1959).
Deane, Herbert A., *The Political and Social Ideas of St. Augustine* (New York, Columbia University Press, 1963).
d'Entreves, Passerin, *Natural Law* (London, Hutchinson's University Library, 1951).
——, *The Case for Natural Law Re-examined* (Notre Dame, Indiana, 1956).
Ebenstein, William, *The Pure Theory of Law* (Madison, University of Wisconsin Press, 1945).
Ehrlich, Eugen, *Fundamental Principles of the Sociology of Law,* trans. W. L. Moll (Cambridge, Harvard University Press, 1936).
Emery, Lucilius, *Concerning Justice* (New Haven, Yale University Press, 1914).
Friedman, W., *Legal Theory* (London, Stevens & Sons, Ltd., 1944).
Friedrich, Carl, *The Philosophy of Law in Historical Perspective* (Chicago, University of Chicago Press, 1958).
Fuller, L. L., "Human Purpose and Natural Law"; Nagel, E., "On the Fusion of Fact and Value: A Reply to Professor Fuller"; and Fuller, L. L., "A Rejoinder to Professor Nagel". *Natural Law Forum,* Vol. 3, No. 1 (1958) 68-104.
——, Cf. entry under Hart, H. L. A.
Geny, François, *Science et Technique en droit prive positif* (Paris, Recueil Sirey, 1914).
Gierke, Otto, *Natural Law and the Theory of Society, 1500 to 1800,* trans. E. Barker (Boston, Beacon Press, 1934).
Gray, John Chipman, *The Nature and Sources of Law* (New York, Columbia University Press, 1901).
Grotius, Hugo, *De Jure Belli ac Pacis,* trans. W. Whewell (Cambridge, University Press, 1853) (first published 1623-1625).
Haines, Charles G., *The Revival of Natural Law Concepts* (Cambridge, Mass., Harvard University Press, 1930).

Hall, Jerome, *Readings in Jurisprudence* (Indianapolis, Bobbs-Merrill Co., 1938).
Harding, Arthur (editor), *Natural Law and Natural Rights* (Dallas, Southern Methodist University Press, 1955).
——, (ed.), *Origins of the Natural Law Tradition* (Dallas, Southern Methodist University Press, 1954).
Hart, H. L. A. and Honore, A. M., *Causation in the Law* (Oxford, Clarendon Press, 1959).
Hart, H. L. A., *The Concept of Law* (Oxford, Clarendon Press, 1961).
——, "Positivism and the separation of Law and Morals"; Fuller, L. L., "Positivism and fidelity to law — a reply to Professor Hart", *Harvard Law Review*, Vol. 71 (2/58), 593.
Hart, Heber L., *The Way to Justice* (London, George Allen and Unwin, Ltd., 1941).
Hegel, *Philosophy of Right*, trans. T. M. Knox (Oxford, Oxford University Press, 1958) (first published 1821).
Heraclitus, *Fragments in Ancilla to the Pre-Socratic Philosophers*, trans. Kathleen Freeman (Oxford, Basil Blackwell, 1956).
Hexner, Erwin, *Studies in Legal Terminology* (Chapel Hill, University of North Carolina Press, 1941).
Hobbes, Thomas, *Leviathan* (New York, Bobbs-Merrill Co., 1958) (first published 1651).
Holmes, O. W., *The Mind and Faith of Justice Holmes*, ed. Max Lerner (Boston, Little, Brown & Co., 1943).
Honore. A. M., Cf. entry under Hart, H. L. A.
Ihering, Rudolf von, *Law as a Means to an End* (New York, Macmillan Co., 1924).
Jenks, Edward, *Law and Politics in the Middle Ages* (New York, Henry Holt & Co., 1912).
Jolowicz, H. F., *Historical Introduction to the Study of Roman Law* (Cambridge, University Press, 1932).
Kant, *The Metaphysics of Ethics - Philosophy of Law*, ed. Semple (Edinburgh, Clark, 1836) (first published 1796).
Kelsen, Hans, *General Theory of Law and State* (New York, Russell & Russell, 1961).
——, *Peace Through Law* (Chapel Hill, University of North Carolina Press, 1944).
——, "The Pure Theory of Law", *Law Quarterly Review*, Vol. 50 (1934).
——, "The Pure Theory of Law and Analytical Jurisprudence", *Harvard Law Review* (1941) 44.
Kennedy, Walter B., "Pragmatism as a Philosophy of Law", *Marquette Law Review*, Vol. 9 (1925).
Korkunov, N. M., *General Theory of Law*, trans. W. G. Hastings (New York, Macmillan Co. (1909) 1922).
Mill, John Stuart, *Utilitarianism* (New York, Liberal Arts Press, Inc., 1957) (first published 1861).
Mitchell, E. T., "Social Ideals and the Law", *Philosophical Review*, Vol. 46 (1937).

Montesquieu, *The Spirit of Laws* (Dublin, G. and A. Ewing, 1751) (first published 1748).
Nagel, E., Cf. entry under Fuller, L. L.
Nussbaum, Arthur, *A Concise History of the Law of Nations* (New York, Macmillan Co., 1954).
Paton, George Whitecross, *A Text-book of Jurisprudence* (Oxford, Clarendon Press, 1951).
Plato, *Laws,* In the *Dialogues of Plato,* Vol. II, trans. B. Jowett (New York, Random House, 1937).
Pollock, Sir Frederick, *Essays in the Law* (London, Macmillan & Co., 1922).
Pound, Roscoe, *An Introduction to the Philosophy of Law* (New Haven, Yale University Press, 1961).
——, *Justice According to Law* (New Haven, Yale University Press, 1951).
——, *Law and Morals* (Chapel Hill, University of North Carolina Press, 1926).
——, *Outlines of Lectures on Jurisprudence* (Cambridge, Harvard University Press, 1943).
——, "The Ideal Element in American Judicial Decision", *Harvard Law Review,* Vol. 45 (1931).
Radbruch, Gustav, *Rechtsphilosophie* (Leipzig, Quelle & Meyer, 1932).
Rommen, Heinrich A., *The State in Catholic Thought* (St. Louis, B. Herder Book Co., 1945).
Rousseau, Jean Jacques, *The Social Contract* (New York, Hafner Publishing Co., 1957) (first published 1762).
Schoch, M., ed., *The Jurisprudence of Interests* (Cambridge, Harvard University Press, 1948).
Stone, Julius, *The Province and Function of Law* (Cambridge, Harvard University Press, 1950).
Strauss, Leo, *The Political Philosophy of Hobbes* (Chicago, The University of Chicago Press, 1952).
St. Thomas Aquinas, *Summa Theologica, Great Books,* Vol. 20 (Chicago, Encyclopaedia Britannica, Inc., 1952).
University of Notre Dame Natural Law Institute Proceedings, Vol. II (Notre Dame, College of Law, 1949).
Wasserstrom, Richard, "Disobeying the Law", *Journal of Philosophy,* Vol. 58, No. 21 (10/12/61), 641-653.
Williams, Glanville L., "A Controversy Concerning the Word Law", *British Yearbook of International Law* (1945) 146.

INDEX

Aquinas, St. Thomas 131-132
Aristotle 127-128
Augustine, St. 130
Austin, John 104 *n*

Bellarmine 132

Ceremonial law. *See* Divine law, positive
Cicero 129
Civil law
  application of 90, 92-93, 97, 119
  as a command of the sovereign 9-11 *pass.*, 13-15, 17-18, 25-26, 27-28, 75, *85-88, 105-107,* 109
  as a plan of life 10-11 *pass.*, 13-14, 25, 75, 107
  as good or evil 74-75, 76, 78, 79, 80, 82-83, 93-95, 101-104, 106-107, 109-110, 112-113
  as regulating behavior 9-11 *pass.*, 13-15, 16, 25-27, 33, 48-49, 73, 78 95-97, 119
  as related to human reason 15, 19-20, 22-24, 27, 31-33, 50-51, 82, 104, *106-107*
  content of 74, 91, *95-97*, 98, 108, 111-113, 119
  efficacy of 15-20, 24, *25-27*, 33, 72-73, *74-75,* 77-80, 82-83, 97, 112, 117-119, 124
  end of *75-76,* 82, *88-99, 116-120*
  evaluation of *100-104, 106-107,* 108-110
  function of, in the state 74, 76, 82, 94, 102, 104, 105, 117, 124

fundamental laws 28, 88, 111, 114-115
interpretation of 29, 90, 90 *n*-91 *n*, 97, *108-110,* 111, 115
jurisdiction of 17-25, 48-49, 50-51, 67, 74, 82-83, *90-92,* 106, *113-116*
justification of 74, *82-83,* 84-86, 95-99
'neutral' laws 91-92
obedience and disobedience to 13, 15-19, *20-24,* 25-27, 32-33, 43, 48-49, 52, 73, 74, 78-80, 81-83, *84-86,* 89, 92-94, 112, 116, 118-119, 120-121
promulgation of 77
relation to higher law 43-44, 48, *72-74, 97-99,* 123
relation to morality 67, 71, 72-74, 76-80, 81-83, *85-86, 88-99,* 101-104, 109-110, 115-116, 121, 121 *n*, 122
sanctions attached 14, 15-20 *pass.*, 26, 74, 76, *79-80,* 89, 96, 118
source of *104-107,* 124
stability and change in *110-113,* 124
validity of *25-27,* 28, 33, 52, *73-75,* 76, *77-84,* 93, 101, 103, 107, 111-112, 116
Civil state. *See also* Civil law
  constitution of 27, 28, 88
  continuance as functional 31-33, 49, 79, 80-81, 84-86, 94
  end and value of 13, 20-24, 31-33, 74-76, 84, 87, *89-95*
  form of 80-81, 97, 111
  goodness of 24, 32, 95

INDEX

moral value of 68, 84, 94-95, 121, 122
origin of 13, 21, 31, 68
pre-civil condition 89-90, 95
proper functions of 18-19, 30, 31, *94-95*
rebellion in 33, 76, 81, *84*
relations with other states 29-30
rights of 20, 21-22, 32, *84-86*
sphere of control 15-20, 22, 24, 49
subjects of: duty and obligation of 18, 20-24, 74, *81, 84-86*, 92, 94, 116-117, 120-121, 121 *n,* 124; relations of 76
Classical command theory of law 14, 104-105, 109
Spinoza's deviations from it 14
Classical natural law theory 14-15, 52-53, 72-73, 91, 105, 109, 110, 116 *n,* 123, 126-135
  Aquinas, St. Thomas 104 *n,* 131-132
  Aristotle, 127-128
  Augustine, St. 130
  Bellarmine 132
  Cicero 129
  Corpus juris 129-130
  Decretum Gratian 130-131
  De Soto 132
  Grotius 133
  Heraclitus 126-127
  Hobbes 133-134
  Plato 127
  Stoics 128
  Suarez 132-133
  Vasquez 132
  Vittoria 132
Common will 26
Corpus Juris 129-140

Decretum Gratian 130-131
De Soto 132
Divine law, natural 9-11, 14, *See also* Divine law, positive, and God, *34-38,* 39, 72
  as necessary principle of existence 10, 11, 14, 34-36, 47
  as related to human law 43-44
  as related to moral law *62-64,* 70-71
  as related to natural law 46-48

objective of 34, 37, 39, 63-64
precepts of 37, 38
Divine law, positive 9, *38-41,* 43, 75, *See also* Divine law, natural
  aim and sanctions of 39, 40
  disobedience of 43
  origin of 39
  sphere of jurisdiction of 39-41, 91, 91 *n*

Ethical considerations *54-71.* See also Moral law, Moral right, Justice
  criteria of virtue *54-56,* 57, 58, 59, *61,* 64, 67-68, *69-71*
  ethics as naturalistic 69
  ethics as objective *69-71*
  meaning of ethical terms 56-58, 70, 77-78, 103
  relativity/objectivity of ethical terms and laws 57, 64, 68-69, 77, 78, *101-104,* 109-110, 123
  self-determination *60-61,* 62-64, 66, 68, *69-70*

God 54, 55-56, 61
  as source of law 9-11 *pass.,* 34-36, 39, 41-42, 43-44, 64
  love of 46-48, 61, 66
  power of 45, 56
  will and understanding of 14, 35-36
Grotius 139

Heraclitus 126-127
Hobbes 7, 26, 51-52, 104 *n,* 133-134
Human law 9-11, *43-44,* 75. *See also* Civil law, Moral law, Divine law, positive
  relation to natural law 48-49
Human nature. *See also* Natural law, of man
  achievement of rationality 15, 19, 20-22, 36-38, 46-48, 58 *n,* 59-62, 64-66, 67, 68-69, 70-71
  as active 58-59, 60-61, 62-64, 66, 69-71
  as determined 45-48, 53, 58, 59-61, 70
  as part of God's intellect 61
  as related to human law 48-49, 89, 105-107, 111

as related to moral theory 57-62, 63, 64-66, 69-71
as responsible 70
as social *64-66*, 68
essence of 59, 61, 66-67, 71
generic traits *69*, 112, 116
motivation of acts of commonwealths 29-30, 49
motivation of individual actions 15-20, 22-24, 26-27, 31-33, 42, 44-49, 50-53, 57, 58-61, 64-66, 67, 68, 74, 77-79, 82, 89, 93, 98-99, 104, 112
powers and rights 50-53, 57-58, 61, 62, 65, 69-71, 93-94, 97
true interests of 15, 18-24, 60-61, 62, *64-66, 70-71*, 78-79

Justice. *See also* Moral law and Moral rights
in the state 75, 97
legal justice *76*, 97, 103, 104, 119
material justice 73, 75, 97, 98
moral justice 102-104
of laws 74, 80, 83, *93-97*, 98, *111-113*, 115, 119

Korkunov 104 *n*

Law in general 9-11, 13-15
Law of nations 29-30
Law of the prophets. *See* Divine law, positive

Moral law 43, *54-71*, 72. *See also* Ethical considerations
as objective 69
meaning of 56-58, 63-64, 78
obedience to 43, 48, 63-64, 67, 73
proper sphere and end of 46, 58-61, 67-69, 90
relation to civil law *88-99*, 109-110
relation to civil state 68, 74, 83, 85-86
relation to higher law 43-44, 46, 48-49, 52-53, 56-62, *62-64*, 69-71, 73-74, 77-78
Moral rights. *See also* Natural right
relation to natural right *52-53*, 80

Natural law 9-11, 14, 41-46. *See also* Classical natural law theory
as different from classical natural law theory 14-15, *52-53, 72-73*, 91, 116, 123
as necessary principles of existence 14, 41-42, *45-48*, 72-74
of man 42-43, *44-46*, 48-49, 50-51, 52-53, 57-62, 69-71, 72, 97-99, 112
relation to civil law 41, 48-49, 73-75, 80, 88, *97-99*, 107, 112, 115-116
relation to moral law 41, 43-44, 56-62, *69-71*, 73-74, 77, 112
relation to natural right 49-50
Natural moral law 14
Natural right 21, *49-53*. *See also* Natural law
in Hobbes 133-134
in the Late Scholastics 132-133
relation to civil law 79-80, 83
relation to morality *52-53*, 80
relation to power *49-52*, 85
Nature, as value neutral 55-56

Plato 127
Power, as characteristic of nature 25, 54
Pragmatic theory 110-111, 111 *n*

Reality. *See* God and Nature
Relations between commonwealths 29-30

Sophists 104 *n*
Sovereign. *See also* Civil law, as a command of the sovereign
as absolute 88, 114-115
duty to subjects and state 23, 74, 76, *85-88*, 107, 116-117, 120-121
function of 95, 115
powers and limits of 26, 27-29, 32-33, 49, 50-52, 88, 106-107, 113-116, 120
self-interest 24, 88
Stoics 128
Suarez 132

Teleological metaphysics 102, 103, 105

Utilitarian theory 110-111

Vasquez 132
Vittoria 132

Will of all 21, 121